Tina Fey

Other books in the People in the News series:

Maya Angelou

Jennifer Aniston

Tyra Banks

David Beckham

Beyoncé

Fidel Castro

Kelly Clarkson

Hillary Clinton

Miley Cyrus

Hilary Duff

Zac Efron

Brett Favre

50 Cent

Al Gore

Tony Hawk

Salma Hayek

LeBron James

Jay-Z

Derek Jeter

Steve Jobs

Dwayne Johnson

Angelina Jolie

Jonas Brothers

Kim Jong Il

Coretta Scott King

Ashton Kutcher

Tobey Maguire

John McCain

Barack Obama

Danica Patrick

Nancy Pelosi

Queen Latifah

Daniel Radcliffe

Condoleezza Rice

Rihanna

J.K. Rowling

Shakira

Tupac Shakur

Will Smith

Gwen Stefani

Ben Stiller

Hilary Swank

Justin Timberlake

Usher

Kanye West

Oprah Winfrey

Tina Fey

by Lauri S. Friedman

LUCENT BOOKS

A part of Gale, Cengage Learning

GALE
CENGAGE Learning™

Detroit • New York • San Francisco • New Haven, Conn • Waterville, Maine • London

GALE
CENGAGE Learning™

LIBRARY OF CONGRESS CATALOGING-IN-PUBLICATION DATA

Friedman, Lauri S.
  Tina Fey / by Lauri S. Friedman.
      p. cm. -- (People in the news)
  Includes bibliographical references and index.
  ISBN 978-1-4205-0238-1 (hardcover)
  1. Fey, Tina, 1970– 2. Television actors and actresses--United States--
Biography. 3. Women television writers--United States--Biography.
4. Women comedians--United States--Biography. I. Title.
  PN2287.F4255 2010
  791.4502'8092--dc22
  [B]
                                                              2009039362

Lucent Books
27500 Drake Rd.
Farmington Hills, MI 48331

ISBN-13: 978-1-4205-0238-1
ISBN-10: 1-4205-0238-7

Printed in the United States of America
1 2 3 4 5 6 7 13 12 11 10 09

Printed by Bang Printing, Brainerd, MN, 1st Ptg., 01/2010

Contents

Foreword

Fame and celebrity are alluring. People are drawn to those who walk in fame's spotlight, whether they are known for great accomplishments or for notorious deeds. The lives of the famous pique public interest and attract attention, perhaps because their experiences seem in some ways so different from, yet in other ways so similar to, our own.

Newspapers, magazines, and television regularly capitalize on this fascination with celebrity by running profiles of famous people. For example, television programs such as *Entertainment Tonight* devote all of their programming to stories about entertainment and entertainers. Magazines such as *People* fill their pages with stories of the private lives of famous people. Even newspapers, newsmagazines, and television news frequently delve into the lives of well-known personalities. Despite the number of articles and programs, few provide more than a superficial glimpse at their subjects.

Lucent's People in the News series offers young readers a deeper look into the lives of today's newsmakers, the influences that have shaped them, and the impact they have had in their fields of endeavor and on other people's lives. The subjects of the series hail from many disciplines and walks of life. They include authors, musicians, athletes, political leaders, entertainers, entrepreneurs, and others who have made a mark on modern life and who, in many cases, will continue to do so for years to come.

These biographies are more than factual chronicles. Each book emphasizes the contributions, accomplishments, or deeds that have brought fame or notoriety to the individual and shows how that person has influenced modern life. Authors portray their subjects in a realistic, unsentimental light. For example, Bill Gates—the cofounder and chief executive officer of the software giant Microsoft—has been instrumental in making personal computers the most vital tool of the modern age. Few dispute his business savvy, his perseverance, or his technical expertise, yet critics say he is ruthless in his dealings with competitors and driven more by his desire to maintain Microsoft's dominance in the computer industry than by an interest in furthering technology.

In these books, young readers will encounter inspiring stories about real people who achieved success despite enormous obstacles. Oprah Winfrey—the most powerful, most watched, and wealthiest woman on television today—spent the first six years of her life in the care of her grandparents while her unwed mother sought work and a better life elsewhere. Her adolescence was colored by promiscuity, pregnancy at age fourteen, rape, and sexual abuse.

Each author documents and supports his or her work with an array of primary and secondary source quotations taken from diaries, letters, speeches, and interviews. All quotes are footnoted to show readers exactly how and where biographers derive their information and provide guidance for further research. The quotations enliven the text by giving readers eyewitness views of the life and accomplishments of each person covered in the People in the News series.

In addition, each book in the series includes photographs, annotated bibliographies, timelines, and comprehensive indexes. For both the casual reader and the student researcher, the People in the News series offers insight into the lives of today's newsmakers—people who shape the way we live, work, and play in the modern age.

A Comedian Makes the News

Tina Fey stands alone in a small world of female comedians. She relies neither on her looks nor sexuality to make a splash, though she has garnered much attention for both. She stays away from typical comedian fodder such as dirty jokes or the differences between men and women, and her comedy has a decidedly "clean" and moral tone to it. Unlike most comedians, Fey is capable of writing, acting, directing, producing, and casting—and conceiving fresh ideas that make people laugh *and* think.

In 2008 Fey became more than just a woman who makes people laugh. She was catapulted from the entertainment headlines to the newspaper headlines when she took on the job of impersonating Alaska governor Sarah Palin, the Republican Party's nominee for vice president. Because of the governor's beauty, small-town background, folksy speaking style, and often bungled statements, she was an easy target for satire. But it was Fey's dead-on impersonation of her that drove Americans of all political persuasions wild and turned "Tina Fey" into a household name.

The "Feylin" Phenomenon

Fey appeared as Palin on six *Saturday Night Live* (*SNL*) sketches in the fall of 2008. In one she appeared with Amy Poehler, who played Democratic presidential hopeful Hillary Clinton, and hilariously asked Americans to stop treating her as a sex symbol. In another Fey spoofed on a series of disastrous interviews the real Palin had given CBS reporter Katie Couric. Fey also played Palin in a mock vice-presidential debate and in a satirical scene that takes place in the White House's oval office. In each of these performances, Fey's mastery of Palin's looks, speech patterns, and mannerisms—not to mention the deadly funny satirical dialogue written mostly by Fey herself—enchanted the American public. "Beyond all reasonable doubt, Sarah Fey and Tina Palin are one,"[1] observed one international reporter.

Immediately, the wildly popular performances crossed over from the headlines of entertainment magazines and were featured in articles in heavy-hitting news sources such as the *New York Times* and the *Los Angeles Times* and on political Web sites like Salon.com and the *Huffington Post*. They led Fey to be voted one of America's ten most fascinating people by Barbara Walters and also as one of the most influential people of the year by *Time* magazine. Her impressions of the Republican vice presidential candidate were credited with shaping the national dialogue about the election and even influencing Americans' votes. A poll conducted by the *Washington Times*, for example, found that a "Tina Fey effect" was turning voters off to both Sarah Palin and her running mate, John McCain. When the two eventually lost the election, many wondered if Tina Fey's performances had hammered the final nail in their coffin.

A Reluctant Political Hero

That the sketches were even being considered to be politically relevant shocked and surprised Fey. The comedian had intended to make a splash, but she had never dreamed she would have any hand in influencing the outcome of the election. The fervor over her appearances on *SNL* during the election season overwhelmed her at times, and she was not entirely comfortable with her new position as the nation's political mouthpiece. She also did not like that people interpreted her comedy bits as her political opinions.

For example, she performed a piece on *Saturday Night Live's* "Weekend Update" segment in which she defended Hillary Clinton, who at the time rivaled black candidate Barack Obama to be the Democratic presidential nominee. The election at this point

Tina Fey appears as Sarah Palin in a Saturday Night Live sketch with John McCain. Fey never expected to have so much political influence with her Sarah Palin performance.

was exciting because never before had a woman and an African American battled for a presidential nomination. After Fey's performance, the country seized on the comments she made during the segment, using them to champion the idea of a female presidential candidate. But Fey had done the segment as a joke—she had not intended the nation to take the bit so seriously. Also, Fey was perceived as being Hillary's number one fan, a title she was uncomfortable with because she was not necessarily a Clinton supporter.

While Fey immensely enjoyed playing Sarah Palin, she was surprised that people took her performances to mean that she somehow disliked the Alaska governor. She claims to hold real respect for Sarah Palin, saying, "That lady is a media star. She is a fascinating person. She's very likable. She's fun to play."[2] Fey approached the imitations of the governor as pure comedy and never intended for Americans to infer that she was trying to influence the outcome of the election with any of her performances.

"The New Woman Who Can Have It All"

But in the fury that led up to the election, Fey's sketches seemed to take on a life of their own. Her performances showed the extent to which entertainment can influence the most important issues of the day. Interestingly, even without the Palin sketches, Fey had already developed a large following through her realistic, unique, and varied portrayals of women. Indeed, unlike many female comedians, Fey has tackled the subjects of infertility and sexism and, through her characters, has realistically portrayed the hardships of being a single, professional woman who has to contend with tough, male-centric environments. She has written these challenging experiences into her characters' lives in a way that few other female entertainers have thought to do. For this reason, "Tina really is the new woman who can have it all," says Donna Langley of Universal Studios. "She's crossed all these barriers and milestones as a woman, so it makes her a great role model."[3]

Perhaps what also makes Fey a great role model is that she does not see herself as one. In fact, she remains a modest, humble, hard worker whose biggest goals in life are to spend time with her family and tackle interesting, unique projects that will make people laugh and think. She has neither a ladder-climber nor a rock star personality but is more of a "good girl" who likes to enforce and follow rules. In an entertainment era often characterized by reduced morals, slutty attire, and sexually suggestive behavior, Fey has offered herself up as a strong female who is out to prove that women do not have to degrade themselves to get laughs. For this she is not only a standout person in comedy but also a newsworthy one.

Chapter 1

An Improvised Life

Tina Fey was born Elizabeth Stamatina Fey on May 18, 1970, to Donald and Jeanne Fey. She grew up in the Greek and Italian neighborhood of Upper Darby, a suburb of Philadelphia. Her mother was Greek, and her father was German-Scottish, giving Tina a unique cultural background.

Unlike many kids Tina got along well with her parents. They both had a good sense of humor, and she deeply admired them. Her father worked many jobs. He was mainly employed as a grant writer for the University of Pennsylvania, but he also served as a paramedic and wrote mystery novels in his spare time. Tina admired his wide range of skills and his dedication to pursuing his interests. She also respected her mother, a homemaker, for her sharp wit. She fondly remembers spending time around her mother and her mother's friends as they played poker each week. "I loved hanging out with the ladies, because they were very funny, and a little bit mean, and had lots of Entenmann's products,"[4] Fey says.

She has one brother, Peter, who is eight years older than her. Fey has described the age gap between them as being the same as growing up with three parents. Despite their distance in age, Tina and Peter got along well. She counts Peter as one of her earliest comedic influences. He would frequently entertain her by doing reenactments of *Saturday Night Live* sketches, the show that would later launch her into fame. Her mother also had a lively sense of humor and would entertain her children by doing comedy routines around the dinner table.

As a youngster Tina had a vivid and even weird imagination that displayed itself in writing and artwork. For example, when she was about seven years old, she drew a sketch of people walking down a street holding hands. They carried huge chunks of Camembert, Cheddar, and Swiss cheeses, and a caption at the bottom said, "What a friend we have in cheeses!"[5] She also displayed her knack for zesty one-liners early on. "She had a very intelligent humor, not the jokey kind," remembers her brother Peter. "She would zing you and a few seconds later you'd react. Like, 'Did a 14-year-old just say that?'"[6]

As a child Tina was influenced by the popular television shows of the time. She loved to watch comedies like *The Mary Tyler Moore Show* and *Newhart*. *Laverne & Shirley*, *Happy Days*, and *Love Boat* were also favorites of hers. Tina recalls she watched a lot of TV, probably more than the average child of her generation. But her parents did not mind, she says, because they loved comedy, too. She remembers them sneaking her in to see the Mel Brooks movie

Comedies like The Mary Tyler Moore Show *(pictured) influenced Tina Fey with their portrayals of funny, smart women.*

Young Frankenstein, and as a family they loved Marx Brothers movies and even *Saturday Night Live*. "My parents mainly wouldn't let me watch stuff that was either annoying to them, or just garbage," she remembers. For example, "My dad wouldn't let us watch *The Flintstones* if he was home, because he said it was a rip-off of *The Honeymooners*."[7]

Scarred for Life

Though Tina's childhood was overwhelmingly defined by happiness and laughter, she suffered a terribly traumatic event that will haunt her for the rest of her life. When she was five years old, a stranger ran up to her as she was playing in the front yard of her house. The person cut her on the left side of her face with a knife. At first Fey thought someone had marked her with a pen. But when

Lorne Michaels, Tina Fey, Alec Baldwin, and Marci Klein (from left to right) at the Emmy Awards where the show 30 Rock won for outstanding comedy series.

the blood started flowing, she knew it was something much worse. She was slashed from the corner of her mouth up several inches alongside her cheek. The incident left Fey with both physical and emotional scars, and police never were able to identify her attacker.

Tina rarely discusses the scar, which has resulted in a lot of mystery. For years reporters speculated about its cause, and a whole Web site called Tina Fey Scar Detective was even devoted to figuring out clues about what had happened to her. Finally, Fey discussed it publicly for the first time in a 2009 interview published in *Vanity Fair*, saying only that as a child, she did not feel any less attractive because of the scar. "I proceeded unaware of it. I was a very confident little kid. It's really almost like I'm kind of able to forget about it, until I was on-camera, and it became a thing." As for why she does not discuss it in more detail or more often, Fey just says, "It's impossible to talk about it without somehow seemingly exploiting it and glorifying it."[8]

Though she herself has commented minimally on the attack, others close to her have speculated on how they think it has affected both her personality and her work. "I think it really informs the way she thinks about her life," said her husband, Jeff Richmond. "When you have that kind of thing happen to you, that makes you scared of certain things, that makes you frightened of different things, your comedy comes out in a different kind of way, and it also makes you feel for people."[9] In his opinion Fey's penchant for humor might spring from her desire to find the humor in even our darkest and saddest experiences.

Another person who has talked with Fey about the experience is Marci Klein, an executive producer of Fey's show, *30 Rock*, and the daughter of fashion designer Calvin Klein. When she was eleven years old, Klein was kidnapped for a day, and Fey felt a kinship over their shared traumas. After hearing of Klein's experience, Fey reportedly reached out to her, saying, "Well, you know, Marci, we had the Bad Thing happen to us. We know what it's like."[10]

Though Tina herself is tight-lipped about the slashing incident, she has alluded to it in the writing she has done for her show, *30 Rock*. Her character, Liz Lemon, is much like Fey—sarcastic and even a little mean at times. After hearing one of her famously sharp quips, her boss tells her, "I don't know what happened in your life that caused you to develop a sense of humor as a coping mechanism. Maybe it was some sort of brace or corrective boot you wore during childhood, but in any case I'm glad you're on my team."[11] It is possible that in writing these lines, Fey was trying to tell the world a little about the early experience that shaped her personality so significantly.

The Original Mean Girl

After recovering from the slashing incident, Tina attended Cardington Elementary School and Beverly Hills Middle School, both in Upper Darby. As early as fifth grade, she was relying on humor as a way to make friends. "I figured out that I could ingratiate myself to people by making them laugh. Essentially, I was just trying to make them like me," she says. "But after a while it became part of my identity."[12] She also used humor as a distraction and a self-defense mechanism. She remembers how in the eighth grade she wrote a note to her math teacher that apologized for making jokes so often in class, and she admitted it was because she struggled with the subject.

As a student at Upper Darby High School, Fey continued to exhibit clear signs of the intelligent but biting personality that has defined her career. Fey remembers being mean in high school—not because she was a nasty or cruel person, but because she felt intimidated by her classmates and even envied some of them. "Technically, I was a jealous girl," she has said. "But because I was jealous, I was mean."[13] She made friends with a group of smart, nerdy students who all took advanced placement (AP) classes. From a safe distance in the lunchroom, they made up biting nicknames for their peers who were prettier or more athletic than them. For example, she and her friends called the preppy, pretty, popular girls the "Laura Ashley Parade" after the fashion designer and the long-haired drinkers in the party crowd the "Hammers" because of the crazy physical stunts they pulled at parties.

Fey remembers nicknaming the prettiest girl in her school "Banana-Boat Boobs" because of the enviable shape and size of her breasts. "I know that was really scraping the bottom of the barrel, insult-wise," she says. "But I was super-jealous of her, and dealt with it by being sarcastic behind her back."[14] Interestingly, Fey's mean streak had a moral aspect to it, and she directed the worst of her ridicule at students who drank or took drugs, ditched classes, dressed inappropriately for school, or who were promiscuous.

Perhaps it was her intelligence that made Fey feel she had the right to make fun of other people; perhaps it was a lack of confidence she had in her own abilities. In fact, it is possible that Fey preyed on pretty girls because she herself felt insecure about her looks. "I had a pretty rough puberty," she remembers. "Growing up as a girl is always traumatizing, especially when you have the deadly combination of greasy skin and getting your [breasts] at ten."[15] Either way, her knack for satirizing her classmates would evolve into a career of making fun of others. Her own experiences in high school later informed her work on *Mean Girls*, a movie about how vicious high school girls can be to one another. As an adult, Fey realizes she was mean to others because she and her friends were insecure about themselves. "We thought we were super cool but we were our own sad little clique,"[16] she once admitted.

A High School Writer

Despite her mean and jealous streak, Fey was a good kid. She was an honors student who took mostly high-level AP classes. Looking back, she compares herself to Lisa Simpson, a brainy, know-it-all type who never drank, did drugs, had sex, or got into any trouble. She rarely had boyfriends, and when she did they were always nice, good boys who never got away with much. "I was so obedient," she says, "someone should do a study of my parents and find out whatever it was they did."[17] Because she always finished her work so quickly, she had lots of time to load up her schedule with tons of extracurricular activities. She was a staff member of the *Oak*, the school's yearbook. She also sang with the group the Encore Singers and performed in many school musicals and plays.

Her biggest high school pastime, though, was writing. She was editor for the school's newspaper, the *Acorn*, and in that position

Second City

The Second City acting troupe was started in the 1950s by undergraduates at the University of Chicago. The group's title comes from a 1952 *New Yorker* article about Chicago. The group puts on shows, or revues, that feature a mix of improvised and scripted sketches. Each revue also features a second act in which actors perform completely improvised scenes that are based on suggestions and ideas from audience members.

Second City has launched the careers of many notable actors. Jeremy Piven (*Entourage*) was with the group in 1988, as was Mike Myers (*Wayne's World, Austin Powers, Shrek*). Steve Carell, of *The 40-Year-Old Virgin* and *The Daily Show*, joined the group in 1991, as did Jeff Garlin (*Curb Your Enthusiasm*). Stephen Colbert, of *The Colbert Report* and *The Daily Show*, was with the group in 1993 and was originally hired to be Carell's understudy. Though not all Second City alumni go on to enjoy such luminous careers, the group is considered to be a hotbed of creativity and a pool of serious talent for network producers to pull from when they cast sitcoms and movies.

Members of the improvisational group Second City rehearse for a performance. Second City has launched the careers of many famous actors.

wrote a regular satire column. She did not use her real name, but wrote her columns under the pseudonym "the Colonel," a pun on the paper's title. Using a pseudonym made Fey feel safe to deliver scathing criticisms of her school environment, and she frequently wrote satirically about school policy and teachers. But she sometimes got in trouble for her biting comments—Fey remembers that one time, "I got busted because I was trying to say that something would 'go down in the annals of history,' but it was a double-entendre with 'anal' and I didn't get away with it."[18]

Writing as the Colonel was one of the activities that convinced Fey she wanted to go into comedy. She says she knew she wanted to be a comedian starting in the eighth grade when, as a reward for finishing her classroom work early, she and another student were allowed to do an independent study project on a topic of their choosing. "She chose to do hers on communism, and I chose to do mine on comedy,"[19] Fey says. In all, Fey's high school experiences with mockery, writing, and theater groomed her well for her future life in improvisational satirical comedy. She left high school on the defensive, sardonic note that defined her time there, writing in the yearbook that in ten years she was likely to be "very, very, fat." She explained: "I was just trying to cover my bases. If I did turn out to be a pudgy loser, I'd be able to say, 'See, I *told* you.'"[20]

The College Years

After graduating from high school in 1988, Fey moved to Charlottesville, Virginia, to attend the University of Virginia. Charlottesville was a totally new and different environment for the Pennsylvania native. Fey was enamored with the distinctly Southern, genteel atmosphere—and the overwhelming number of blondes she encountered everywhere. She originally majored in English because of her natural interest in and talent for writing. However, she quickly left the department, claiming it was too snobbish for her tastes. She switched her major to her second love—drama—and promptly became a self-described theater nerd.

Fey recalls dressing outside the mainstream, favoring black tights, Doc Martens, and baby-doll dresses. As a college student she continued to nurture her sarcastic mean streak, making fun of the typical university types around her. She also maintained her good-girl ways: Although she went to parties famous for their kegs, she never drank. She also preferred to live on campus for longer than most students, reportedly to be close to the university's theater.

It was during her years in Virginia that she started to write scripts and comedy bits, learning skills that would provide the foundation of her career. She also performed in several theatrical productions, holding notable roles. As a senior she played Sally Bowles, the lead role in the musical *Cabaret*. She also frequently performed a monologue from a Tennessee Williams play called *This Property Is Condemned*. Unlike many college students who spent their summers working odd jobs or traveling, Fey spent the months off from the university involved with Summer Stage theater productions. She sang and acted in some performances and spent two summers as a director.

Second City, Second Life

Many students graduate from college unsure about what direction to follow in life—but not Fey. After graduating from the University of Virginia in 1992, she immediately moved to Chicago, where she took classes from the illustrious improvisational comedy troupe, Second City. Second City is known for churning out dozens of great comedians—and many future *Saturday Night Live* alumni—such as John and James Belushi, Bill Murray, Dan Aykroyd, Mike Myers, Chris Farley, Tim Meadows, Rachel Dratch, Adam McKay, and Amy Poehler. In fact, the whole reason Fey was interested in Second City was because, as she explained, "I knew it was where a lot of 'SNL' people had started."[21] Through the group Fey took improv classes and acting workshops. While she honed her craft, she supported herself with a job in child care at the local YMCA. In order to keep her evenings free to take improv classes, she worked the 5:30 A.M. to 2:00 P.M. shift there.

In 1994, after two years in training, she was invited to join the group as an understudy in their touring ensemble. She toured for a little less than a year and eventually began performing on their main stage. In this position she wrote and performed monologues,

The Art of Improvisational Theater

Known as "improv" or "impro," improvisational theater uses specific techniques to create spontaneous, unrehearsed performances. Many improv troupes take suggestions from the audience to create a setting and plot for the sketch. To be a successful improv actor, one must be a good listener, have extreme confidence, and possess instinctual performing skills.

Improv theater is believed to date back to Europe in the 1500s. In places such as Italy, street performers used improv techniques to entertain crowds and earn money. It became a more formalized technique in the late 1800s when directors began using improv to train and rehearse actors. In the twentieth century improv games became heavily featured in high school theater classrooms and even as a part of corporate training programs to encourage employees to open up and build trust among one another.

Modern improv is considered to have been born with Viola Spolin, who trained the first generation of improv actors in troupes such as the Compass Players and Second City. More

recently the technique has been worked into mockumentary films such as *This Is Spinal Tap* and *Best in Show* and reality television–esque shows such as HBO's *Curb Your Enthusiasm*.

A July 5, 1955, photo shows the first performance of "The Compass," a University of Chicago–based improvisational comedy troupe.

sketches, and one-act plays. She held this position for about a year and a half. As a Second City performer, Fey stood out not just for being funny, but for being a funny *female*. Remembers Richmond, her husband: "I don't want to say she was funny 'for a woman,' but there were so many talented men there at the time, and then suddenly there was Tina, who was so funny—and she was at home with all those boys on the stage."[22]

Learning the craft of improvisation helped acting make sense to Fey. She describes it as helping her body and emotions become free enough to truly channel a character, rather than just imitate it. Furthermore, the go-with-the-flow aspect of improv appealed to Fey and helped guide her in her day-to-day offstage life. "I've

Pseudonyms

A pseudonym (also called a pen name) is a fake name used by a writer to disguise his or her identity. Like Tina Fey, many well-known writers have used a pen name at some point in their career. One of the most famous pseudonyms is "Mark Twain," which was the pen name of writer Samuel Clemens.

Writers have various reasons for using a pen name. In the days when it was frowned upon for women to write distinguished works of literature, female authors would use male pen names to get their work published. A well-known example is the writer Mary Ann Evans, who wrote under the name George Eliot. Other female authors who used pen names include Jane Austen and the Brontë sisters. Other writers may want to distinguish their literary writing from other work. This was the reasoning behind mathematician Charles Dodgson's decision to write fiction under the name Lewis Carroll. Today writers use pen names to protect their identity (for example, if they are writing sensitive political material) or to see whether audiences will still like their work even if unconnected to their name. This is the reason author Stephen King has published several novels under the name Richard Bachman.

found the general philosophy of it to be quite helpful," she says. "It reminds me that if I stumble onto something unexpected in my writing, something that I didn't anticipate or intend, I should be willing to follow it."[23]

By 1997 it seemed that Fey had accomplished everything she set out to do—she was performing improv comedy on a nightly basis with one of the most renowned comedy troupes in the country. She had met her future husband, a levelheaded, moral Midwesterner who was a good match for her good-girl style—and, as a piano player for another Chicago-based improv troupe, shared her love for the improvisational arts. Although Fey had been drawn to Second City as a route to *Saturday Night Live*, she quickly came to love the improvisational life for its own merits. "I became immersed in the cult of improvisation," she said. "I was so sure that I was doing exactly what I'd been put on this earth to do, and I would have done anything to make it onto that stage. Not because of *SNL*, but because I wanted to devote my life to improv."[24] She says that she would have been perfectly content to stay at Second City for the rest of her life, turning into an old woman there. But Fey was about to make a bold move that would change her life forever, taking her to heights she had never dreamed possible.

Chapter 2

Live from New York, It's Tina Fey

When Fey was twenty-seven years old, she thought she was living life at the top. But in June 1997, she made a decision that would catapult her to even greater heights. It started when her friend Adam McKay urged her to send some sample scripts to Lorne Michaels, *Saturday Night Live's* powerful and charismatic executive producer. Fey knew McKay from his work at Second City, and since then he had gone on to be head writer at *Saturday Night Live*. McKay thought Fey was perfect for *SNL*—and after reading her samples, so did Michaels. Within just a couple of months of receiving the scripts, he offered her a job as a staff writer on the show.

Fey initially paused when presented with this intimidating yet awesome opportunity. On the one hand, she had been interested in doing sketch comedy since she was a little girl, and *Saturday Night Live* was the apex of that universe. On the other hand, at Second City she was able to write and perform comedy seven days a week in a personal, intimate environment. She was also in love with Jeff Richmond, the piano player with whom she had begun an intense relationship. Above all, she loved the city of Chicago—it felt like home. But when she told friend Amy Poehler (a future *Saturday Night Live* cast member) about the opportunity— and about the salary Michaels had offered her—Poehler strongly urged her to take the job.

Once Fey dug in to *SNL's* quirky backstage atmosphere and close community of writers, she never looked back. "I'd had my eye on the show forever, the way other kids have their eye on Derek Jeter," she said. She enjoyed the rowdy, intense atmosphere of the writers' room. It was always crowded and noisy, with writers constantly bouncing jokes and potential bits off each other. It perhaps is not surprising that in an office packed with some of the most talented writers and actors of the day, Fey was always greeted with hilarious antics and off-the-wall pranks. "Most of the time you're too busy to think about it, but every now and then you say, 'I work at *Saturday Night Live*,' and that is so cool,"[25] she said. Also, she was able to salvage a long-distance relationship with Richmond, and within a few years he ended up getting a job at *SNL*, too, as a composer of music for skits.

Writer Adam McKay on the set of the movie Step Brothers. *McKay helped Tina Fey get her start on* Saturday Night Live *by urging her to send some sample scripts to executive producer Lorne Michaels.*

Lorne Michaels

Lorne Michaels is the charismatic and highly imitable creator and producer of *Saturday Night Live*. Michaels has mentored many of the *Saturday Night Live* comedians who have gone on to make their own movies, such as Adam Sandler, Rob Schneider, Tina Fey, and Mike Myers. As a result, many characters in their films have been based loosely on him. The most famous of these is Dr. Evil in the *Austin Powers* series. The inflection of Dr. Evil's voice, his speech patterns, and his cool, aloof deliveries are all direct reflections of Michaels's personality. Other movies and television shows that have featured characters based in part on Michaels include *Scrooged*, *Brain Candy*, and Fey's *30 Rock*.

As the creator and producer of Saturday Night Live, Lorne Michaels *has helped create many big stars.*

"If She Laughs, Everyone's Laughing"

Fey found life at *SNL* invigorating but also challenging. The show's weekly schedule was grueling—writers had but days to come up with funny bits, and these had to go over well with numerous people before they were ever showed to an audience. Fey remembers that for her first show, she wrote a sketch about then president Bill Clinton that did not get any laughs from the other writers when it was previewed. "This weight of embarrassment came over me, and I felt like I was sweating from my spine out," she says. "But I realized, 'Okay, that happened, and I did not die.'"[26] From the experience she learned it is important to experience failure, understand why one failed, and then move past it.

After just two years as a staff writer, Fey was promoted to head writer in 1999—the first female head writer in the show's history. In this coveted position Fey was responsible for writing two sketches a week and for heading up a "rewrite table," where other writers had to preview their sketches for criticism. She was known for being fair but tough in this role, and producer Michaels appreciated her ability to know when to let go of an idea that had become stale or cold. As a result of these qualities, Fey commanded the attention and respect of the other writers and performers. *SNL* actor Jimmy Fallon said other cast members deferred to her in terms of which sketches to drop and which to pursue. Said Fallon, "If she laughs, everyone's laughing."[27]

Fey also landed herself a spot in a select group of writers who ultimately decided which sketches would air, and as such was in the position of determining the direction of each show's content. In addition, she was given the ability to hire and fire other writers. She used her power to add more funny females to the cast. In fact, women such as Amy Poehler, Rachel Dratch, and Maya Rudolph all landed their spots on *Saturday Night Live* in part because of Fey (who knew Poehler and Dratch from her time in Chicago).

Fey's dramatic—and fast—success on the show led some to complain that executive producer Michaels was playing favorites with her, and some even speculated the two were having an affair. But the truth was that Michaels just saw immense talent in

Fey and was proud to showcase it. Said Michaels: "There's a group of people who feel Tina can do no wrong in my eyes. But that's because she's just wrong less often than other people."[28]

A Female Force to Be Reckoned With

As a head writer Fey penned interesting, funny sketches that boosted the ratings of a dying show. She also brought a feminist dynamic to an entertainment institution that had a die-hard reputation for being an "old boy's club." Indeed, at that time the majority of the show's superstars over its two decades of existence had been men, and the majority of the writers were male, too. Females who tried to insert themselves into this atmosphere had found it a difficult, even chauvinistic place to work. For example, comedian Janeane Garofalo, who spent just a few months on the show in the mid-1990s, famously criticized the male-dominated environment in *Live from New York: An Uncensored History of Saturday Night Live*, an official history of the show. Garofalo said she hated the working environment so much that she wanted to quit after her first week. But when Fey took over, even though Garofalo did not work there anymore, the changes were apparent to her. "With the Tina Fey regime, things started turning around," she said. "I think the prevailing attitude had been that women just aren't quite as funny."[29]

Fey was able to insert gender humor into sketches in a way that the show's male writers were uncomfortable doing. For example, Fey took on spoofs about feminine hygiene products, infertility, sexual abuse, and plastic surgery. Fey remembers a time when a male staff member asked her if she thought her sketches were "anti-woman." Fey said it was her job to make fun of people, and including women in that group made her an equal-opportunity comedian.

In fact, Fey is a self-proclaimed feminist, but she considers women fair game if a joke made about them is truthful. "You can't be afraid to write comedy about women, because then you're just going to perpetuate the idea that women aren't as big a part of society [as men are]," she says. The trick, in Fey's eyes, is to write

Amy Poehler, Ana Gasteyer, Hugh Jackman, Maya Rudolph, and Rachel Dratch (from left to right) appear in an opening monologue sketch on **Saturday Night Live.** *As head writer for the show, Tina Fey penned funny sketches with a feminist dynamic.*

about women as she sees them. For example, "I'm not going to write a sketch where [former first lady and Secretary of State] Hillary Clinton is a raving, ball-busting, secret lesbian, because that's not my perception of her," she says. "I've written things where she was the furious, put-upon wife of an adulterer, but the tone is much different because a woman is writing it."[30]

Yet despite a reputation for being feminist, derogatory words for women worked their way into noticeably more *SNL* sketches as soon as Fey became head writer. Fey considers use of these terms appropriate for a woman to use when writing about other women. She feels the fact that she is a woman allows her to use such words in the same way that black comedians are often best suited for making jokes about African Americans. "It's like black people can use 'the n-word' and white people should not," she says. "It's a little bit. . . . It's between us."[31]

From the Writer's Desk to the "Weekend Update" Desk

Fey made the transition from writer to actor after Michaels saw her perform in a comedy sketch at the Upright Citizens Brigade Theatre, a popular comedy venue in New York. Michaels encouraged her to audition for the coanchor position on the "Weekend Update" segment of the show, where each week two anchors make light of the week's news events. Anchoring "Weekend Update" is a particularly demanding role on *SNL*. To make sure the jokes are as up-to-date as possible, the writing for the segment is always done last—sometimes even just hours before the show airs.

Fey cohosted "Weekend Update" with fellow *SNL* star Jimmy Fallon from 2000 to 2004. From 2004 to 2006 she cohosted the desk with Amy Poehler, making it the first time in the show's history that two women anchored the segment. Throughout her time behind the "Weekend Update" desk, viewers enjoyed her characteristic short, sharp barbs and smart, spirited rants into the camera. Even though she left the show in 2006 to pursue other interests, she continued to make guest appearances in *SNL* sketches and on "Weekend Update." In fact, by the end of the 2008–2009 season, Fey had made the most appearances on "Weekend Update" of any anchor of the segment. She had appeared on the program 118 times, followed by Dennis Miller (who has appeared 111 times), Poehler (81 times), and Fallon and Jane Curtin (who have each appeared 80 times).

The Ugly Duckling Turns Glamour-Puss Swan

Fey underwent an incredible transformation when she came out from behind the writer's desk to star on *Saturday Night Live*. At the time she was being considered for "Weekend Update," she was overweight and rather frumpy looking. She did not tweeze her eyebrows; she did not condition her hair. She hid beneath long skirts and bulky sweaters and reportedly favored wearing a ski hat while she wrote. She munched on junk food as she slaved away over scripts, and Fey estimates she weighed close to 150

Making News on "Weekend Update"

The "Weekend Update" segment first aired on October 11, 1975, on the very first *Saturday Night Live* broadcast. It was originally anchored by Chevy Chase, who famously closed the broadcast with his signature statement, "Good night, and have a pleasant tomorrow." "Weekend Update" is *Saturday Night Live*'s longest-running sketch and is often credited as being one of the first programs to launch the now-popular satirical news format. Indeed, since "Weekend Update" first aired, fake or comedic news shows have become increasingly popular and include shows such as *The Daily Show with Jon Stewart, The Colbert Report, The Showbiz Show* with David Spade, and other fake news shows or segments within shows.

As of 2009 the "Weekend Update" desk had been anchored by thirty-two people. Notable anchors include Chevy Chase, Dennis Miller, Kevin Nealon, Norm Macdonald, Colin Quinn, Jimmy Fallon, Tina Fey (who, as anchor, brought back Chase's famous closing quip in her sign-off statements), Amy Poehler, and Seth Meyers. In 2009 it was reported that NBC had plans to turn the "Weekend Update" segment into a thirty-minute prime-time television series.

Buck Henry and Chevy Chase (right) on "Weekend Update." Tina Fey mimicked Chase's closing quip during her stint as a "Weekend Update" coanchor.

pounds (68kg) at this point, which was too much for her petite 5-foot-4-inch (162.56cm) frame.

Those she worked with did not originally see her as the knock-out she is now commonly viewed as being. "When she got here she was kind of goofy-looking,"[32] said Steve Higgins, one of *Saturday Night Live*'s producers. Hollywood agent Sue Mengers remembers one night when Michaels brought Fey over to Mengers's house to see what she thought of casting Fey in "Weekend Update." "She was very mousy," remembers Mengers, who warned Michaels against putting her on camera. "She doesn't have the looks."[33]

Richmond also remembers Fey's pre–"Weekend Update" style, although with more appreciation than others. "She was quite round, in a lovely, turn-of-the-century kind of round." He also says her sense of style left much to be desired. She favored mis-matched outfits and awkward, garish footwear. "She would wear

Tina Fey appears with Jimmy Fallon on "Weekend Update." Before her television debut, Fey lost weight and revamped her wardrobe

just a lot of knee-length frumpy dresses with thrift-store sweaters and kind of what was comfortable,"[34] he says.

A turning point came for Fey shortly before she auditioned for the coanchor spot on "Weekend Update." She remembers catching a glimpse of herself on a monitor around the studio, "and I was like, 'Ooogh.' I was starting to look unhealthy. I looked like a behemoth, a little bit."[35] It was at this point that Fey started Weight Watchers and dropped 30 pounds (13.6kg). Once the weight came off, she became interested in fashion and started dressing in more fashionable outfits. In a short while she developed the "sexy librarian" look for which she is now renowned. The look is signified by sharp business suits, a smart haircut, and her "hot teacher" glasses.

"The Thinking-Man's Sex Symbol"

The change in Fey was so remarkable that people who had ignored her for years began to take notice. Said one colleague, "Steve Martin [who frequently visited the show, used to walk] right past her at the coffee table, and then, after the makeover, he was like, 'Well, hel-looo—who are you?'"[36] Alec Baldwin, her costar on *30 Rock* and a frequent host of *Saturday Night Live*, has put Fey's transformation in the following way: "The collective consciousness has said, 'Tina, *dahling*, where have you been? Where on earth have you been?'"[37]

Soon it was not just Fey's costars who were noticing her looks. So were viewers and critics everywhere. "Maybe it's the naughty-librarian fantasy," wrote reporter David Hiltbrand, "but guys were looking beyond Fey's glasses and severe business attire at the 'Update' desk and seeing a babe."[38] In 2002 she landed at number 80 on *Maxim* magazine's list of 100 Sexiest Women. The following year she was listed among *People* magazine's 50 Most Beautiful People of the Year. *Rolling Stone* called her "the thinking-man's sex symbol,"[39] and *New Yorker* columnist Michael Specter famously dubbed her as "the sex symbol for every man who reads without moving his lips."[40]

"I think it's really funny and I try to enjoy it," says Fey of the newfound attention to her appearance. "When I was in my early

Amy Poehler

Actress and comedian Amy Poehler has teamed up with Tina Fey on many occasions. The two first met in the early 1990s in Chicago, where they were both studying the art of improvisational acting. Poehler joined the cast of *Saturday Night Live* in 2001, when Fey was already serving as head writer. From 2004 to 2006, the pair hosted *SNL*'s "Weekend Update" desk together, making it the first time in the show's history that two women anchored the segment. The two have also made movies together. Poehler played the role of a trying-to-be-hip mother in Fey's 2004 hit *Mean Girls* and costarred with Fey in the 2008 comedy *Baby Mama*.

But perhaps Poehler and Fey's most notable team accomplishment came in 2008 when they paired up for several *SNL* sketches that mocked events in that year's presidential campaign. In one sketch Fey portrayed Republican vice presidential nominee Sarah Palin while Poehler depicted Democratic presidential hopeful Hillary Clinton. Audiences delighted in Fey's spot-on imitation of Palin and Poehler's wry depiction of Clinton. In another sketch Fey played Palin while Poehler adopted the role of *CBS Evening News* interviewer Katie Couric, who did several memorable interviews with Palin in real life.

Tina Fey and Amy Poehler (right) as Sarah Palin and Hillary Clinton.

twenties, being called sexy was not part of my experience in any way." Fey takes a "ride-it-while-it-lasts" approach to the current obsession with her beauty. She says:

> There's such a small window of time when people want to write *any* articles about you. If you're a woman and they say anything complimentary about your appearance, well, I'm not going to complain. I fully intend to keep all of these magazines in the attic and bring them out for my daughter someday. "You see? There was a time when people thought your mother was . . . sexy."[41]

Fey Takes *SNL* to the Top

Once behind the "Weekend Update" desk, geek-turned-glamorous Fey brought more than just extra laughs to *Saturday Night Live*. When she joined the show as a writer in 1997, the show had suffered several seasons of critically low ratings. But Fey's work both on and off camera boosted it to heights of popularity it had not seen in nearly a decade. In 2001, the same year she was named one of *Entertainment Weekly*'s Entertainers of the Year, Fey shared a Writers Guild Award with the other writers for her work on the show's twenty-fifth anniversary special. The following year she helped the show win an Emmy for outstanding writing—an award it had not received since 1989. By 2003 *SNL* was the most popular late-night show on television, attracting more viewers than programs like *The Tonight Show with Jay Leno* or *Late Night with David Letterman*.

Fey is modest about her role in this success, saying it was the collective hard work of a talented team and that she just happened to be hired during a time when the show was on an upswing. Yet many credit Fey's snarky, sharp style with single-handedly injecting new life into *SNL* and with carving a new kind of career path for female comedians, actresses, and writers.

Chapter 3

Writing Her Way to the Top

As Fey became more comfortable with both writing and acting, she launched a few personal projects, all of which have become major hits. The first came in 2004 when she tackled the subject of catty high school girls in the movie *Mean Girls*. Two years later she left *Saturday Night Live* to write and star in her own show, *30 Rock*, and followed the show's first season by taking her first starring lead in another movie, *Baby Mama*. All of these endeavors reflect Fey's now-trademark style: sharp, high-quality humor that tends to explore women's issues and experiences.

Queen Bees and Wannabes

Fey's first project outside of *Saturday Night Live* was the movie *Mean Girls*, which is about the merciless world of teenage girls. The film is actually based on a nonfiction book called *Queen Bees and Wannabes: Helping Your Daughter Survive Cliques, Gossip, Boyfriends, and Other Realities of Adolescence*, by Rosalind Wiseman. The book is a sociological look at the various groups teenage girls organize themselves into and was originally written as a handbook for parents. In it Wiseman discusses the different social roles that girls play in high school society. In this "Girl World," Wiseman identifies several different types of girls, such as popular "Queen Bee" types, imitator wannabes, personality-less sidekicks, information-gathering "bankers," and more.

*Tina Fey starred in the movie **Mean Girls**, which is based on a book written by Rosalind Wiseman (pictured).*

Fey first got the idea to adapt the book into a movie after reading an article about the author in the *New York Times Magazine*. The subject matter fascinated her and also reminded her of her own teenage years. She saw the potential for it to be adapted into a fictional screenplay, and so she took the idea to *SNL* producer Lorne Michaels, who frequently backs the movie projects of his actors. He liked the idea, too, and so Fey called the author and requested an advance copy of the book.

At first Wiseman was reluctant. "She basically wanted me to promise her that I wouldn't take her book and make it into a cheap, dumb, dirty movie; [m]ake fun of it or sell it out,"[42] says Fey. But after Fey reassured her that it was the smart tone of the book that interested her, Wiseman agreed to let her turn the book into a movie.

Real-Life *Mean Girl* Experiences

Fey had to get creative when turning the nonfiction book into a fictional movie script. For material Fey took anecdotes from the book and turned them into scenes between fictional characters. Some of the movie's most memorable scenes actually came from Fey's own teenage life and experiences. For example, she really did have a health teacher like the one portrayed by Dwayne Hill. In the movie his character, Coach Carr, takes a misinformed and even bullying approach to sex education. "Don't have sex," his character warns. "You will get pregnant and die. If you touch each other, you will get chlamydia and die."[43] He then proceeds to hand out a bucket of condoms to the classroom of students. Such exaggerated, mixed messages are famous in American high schools, including Fey's own, and her spot-on depiction of them helped the movie resonate with students, parents, and teachers. Fey also based Ms. Norbury, the character she played, on another of her real teachers from high school—her favorite one, her German teacher.

Trying to Be Less Mean

Mean Girls tells the story of cruel high school girls who torment each other out of jealousy and competitiveness. Even though she wrote the movie to show that this behavior is wrong, Tina Fey herself has often been accused of being mean. In high school and college she routinely made fun of people who were different than her, and jokes she wrote for "Weekend Update" have been described by both audiences and colleagues as hard-edged and even cruel.

Fey recognizes she has a sharp mean streak, and has said she'd like to overcome it. "I'm really trying to move away from it," she says. "Because I don't think you can have a long future in that. You can be mean and caustic in your teens and 20s, but if you keep it going, by the time you're 40, you're just going to be a [jerk]. You're just going to be an old [jerk.]"

Quoted in Emily Rems, "Mrs. Saturday Night," *Bust*, Spring 2005, p. 42.

Tina Fey in a scene from **Mean Girls.** *Fey called on memories of her own teenage years to create some of the most memorable scenes in the movie.*

Fey also experienced a relationship similar to the one portrayed by characters Cady Heron (played by Lindsay Lohan) and Aaron Samuels (played by Jonathan Bennett), in which a girl dumbs herself down to try to get the attention of a popular, attractive boy. "[That relationship] was sort of like the fumbling obsessive pursuit that I was trying to do in high school," Fey says. "It never worked out for me." But Fey recognizes that she was not, in reality, very much like Cady at all. "I was somewhere in between the characters of Janice and the mathletes," she says—a little bit nerdy, and also filled with a distinct animosity for prettier, more popular girls in high school. As for which of Rosalind Wiseman's girl categories she best fits into, Fey says, "I was sort of a banker because I was the sort of person where, if there was gossip about someone, I wanted to know all of it in detail and have it, like, ready. The one that freely will pass on the gossip if they hear it."[44] Such girls are also portrayed in the movie.

Fey was also frequently the victim of snide traps like the one that character Regina George (played by Rachel McAdams) sets for Cady. In one scene Regina tells Cady that she thinks Cady is really pretty. Instead of denying or deflecting the compliment like most insecure girls would, Cady thanks her for it. Regina takes Cady's appreciation for the compliment as a mark of arrogance. "So you agree? You think you're really pretty?"[45] Regina asks, putting Cady on the spot and in effect accusing her of being conceited. Fey says she found herself in a similar situation once, and she resented the suggestion that liking something about herself could be a bad thing. She feels such kinds of interactions between girls discourage them from being proud of their beauty, intelligence, or talent. By adding the message to the movie, she hoped to expose the bankruptcy in such interactions and highlight how girls should work together to play up each other's best qualities rather than cutting each other down.

Praise for *Mean Girls*

Fey's work schedule on *Mean Girls* was grueling. In addition to being both a writer and an actor on the project, the movie was shot in Toronto, but Fey was still responsible for appearing on *Saturday Night Live* in New York every weekend. In order to juggle both projects at once, she would finish *SNL* at around 1:00 A.M. on Sunday morning. Then she would take off her makeup, put on pajamas, and get directly into a motor home that shuttled her up to Canada. She would sleep the whole eight-and-a-half-hour drive and be on the set of *Mean Girls* by the morning.

Her efforts were well worth it, though, because *Mean Girls* won acclaim from many reviewers and moviegoers. The film was praised for providing a humorous portrayal of the real-life issues faced by teenage girls without glorifying or promoting them. As one reviewer commented, "'Mean Girls' manages to rail against stereotypes while still trafficking in them."[46] Critic Roger Ebert concurred, saying that the movie stood out in its genre as a quality film that was as entertaining as it was thoughtful. "In a wasteland of dumb movies about teenagers," he wrote, "'Mean Girls' is a smart and funny one. It even contains some wisdom." Calling the screenplay "both a comic and a sociological achievement," Ebert concluded that "'Mean Girls' dissects high school society with a lot of observant detail, which seems surprisingly well-informed."[47]

From a Hit Show to a Show Within a Show

Fey had taken on the challenge of *Mean Girls* as a way of exploring what her career might look like post–*Saturday Night Live*. Encouraged by the success of the movie and emboldened by how much she enjoyed the experience, Fey left *SNL* in 2006 to pursue more of her own writing. The first of these projects was a half-hour situation comedy called *30 Rock*, which is based on Fey's experiences as a writer at *SNL*.

30 Rock is a behind-the-scenes look at the writers and actors of a live variety show called *The Girlie Show*. With its hastily written comedy sketches and live production in New York, *The Girlie Show* bears many resemblances to *Saturday Night Live*. Its main character, Liz Lemon, has much in common with Fey; Lemon is

Alec Baldwin and Tina Fey in a scene from 30 Rock. *The show is based on Fey's experiences as a* Saturday Night Live *writer.*

the head writer of the show and must constantly put up with powerful, insane, or otherwise bothersome men (and sometimes Jenna, *The Girlie Show's* irrational and vain female lead). In spite of the antics of such men, Lemon struggles to keep up the quality of the show and also to keep its writing centered around Jenna's performances. In addition, *The Girlie Show's* producer, played by Alec Baldwin, is based loosely on charismatic and quirky *SNL* producer Lorne Michaels. Finally, the show's name is short for 30 Rockefeller Plaza, the address of the *Saturday Night Live* studios. In addition to creating the show, Fey serves as its head writer, executive producer, and casting director.

Upon first airing, *30 Rock* was well received by critics and reviewers, who found it smart, different, and entertaining. Yet despite its praise, *30 Rock* struggled to attract viewers. For one thing it initially aired on Wednesday nights, which is not a high-viewing night (compared with Thursday nights, for example). Also viewers may have initially found it too similar to another NBC show, *Studio 60 on the Sunset Strip*, which was also a show-about-a-show (and also bears connections to *Saturday Night Live*). Despite its low ratings, *30 Rock* thrived and enjoyed greater success in its subsequent seasons.

Another Movie Project

Shortly after launching *30 Rock*, Fey turned her attention back to the silver screen, teaming up with former *SNL* "Weekend Update" coanchor Amy Poehler in a movie called *Baby Mama*. Fey plays Kate Holbrook, a successful businesswoman in her late thirties who wants to have a baby. Because she has spent so much of her life focused on her career, Kate is facing serious fertility issues. So she hires an obnoxious, low-class woman—Angie Ostrowiski (Poehler)—to be a surrogate mother (a woman who carries a fertilized egg to term in her womb).

Baby Mama was an original addition to the film offerings of the times for several reasons. For one, it is rare to see a comedy that features two female leads. Many of the most popular comedies, such as *Knocked Up, Forgetting Sarah Marshall,* or *Superbad,* are directed by men, feature male leads, and portray events from a

Tina Fey and Amy Poehler (right) appear in a scene from **Baby Mama. Though the movie received mixed reviews, most critics praised Fey and Poehler for their performances.**

male perspective. As reporter Peter Brownfield put it, "It seems unusual—if not illegal—for two females . . . to have the leads in a buddy comedy. . . . It's almost like an experiment in comedy science class: What if these roles went to funny women who've earned their shot at big-screen success?"[48] Secondly, *Baby Mama* covered unique subject matter that does not lend itself to humor right off the bat. In fact, Fey said the subject matter was one of the main reasons she was drawn to the script. "I liked the topicality of the fertility issues that affect so many people," she said. "There's so much weirdness and emotion about it. If you start with something juicy, you end up with a better [movie] than if you just start with some jokes."[49]

Yet *Baby Mama* received mixed reviews from critics. "The visual style is sitcom functional, and even the zippiest jokes fall flat because of poor timing," wrote *New York Times* reviewer Manohla

Dargis. "But, much like the prickly, talented Ms. Fey, [*Baby Mama*] pulls you in with a provocative and, at least in current American movies, unusual mix of female intelligence, awkwardness and chilled-to-the-bone mean."[50] Said another reviewer, "An essentially sweet-natured picture that doesn't go as far as it could."[51]

But no matter what they thought of the movie, almost all reviewers complimented Poehler and Fey for achieving a female comedy team unique to contemporary cinema. "Though the competition hasn't exactly been stiff, Fey and Poehler may well be the best female comedy duo since Lucy and Ethel,"[52] wrote one reviewer. Wesley Morris of the *Boston Globe* agreed. "In this era of [Judd] Apatow and [Will] Ferrell and [Seth] Rogen and [Owen] Wilson, of men monopolizing movie comedy, *Baby Mama* feels absurdly momentous, and even political," he wrote. "Fey and Poehler aren't just taking back control of their bodies. They're taking back control of their profession."[53]

Tina Fey, Meet Sarah Palin

While both *30 Rock* and *Baby Mama* represented interesting new steps in Fey's career, neither captured the nation's attention as much as when she impersonated vice presidential candidate Sarah Palin during the 2008 election season. Palin, then the governor of Alaska, took the country by surprise and storm when she was selected by Republican nominee John McCain to be his running mate.

Palin was an interesting and unusual choice for the ticket. She was a young, attractive woman and stood in exciting contrast to McCain's older, more grandfatherly personality. Because she was from Alaska, Palin was also viewed as being far outside the mainstream of American politics, and she also had unusual hobbies like hunting. But Palin was also criticized as being too inexperienced to fill the position of vice president. She had only served as governor for two years and prior to that had been the mayor of a small Alaskan town.

Yet Palin had a mesmerizing charm that energized all Americans, polarizing them either for or against her. A self-described "hockey mom," Palin frequently delivered her political messages in down-home, folksy English. Some Americans found this appealing and related very well to her "of-the-people" character. Others found her language inappropriate for a politician and even viewed it as a mark against her intelligence. She quickly became known for making spirited, sassy statements that dominated the day's headlines, even if they lacked political substance. For example, she became famous for describing herself and John McCain as a team of "maverick" politicians who intended to shake up American politics; she also famously railed against the "liberal media," which she claimed misrepresented her words. What Palin became most famous for, however, were her long-winded and often blundering answers to questions posed by journalists and others.

"Feylin" Is Born

In every political season, late-night comedy shows make brutal fun of the candidates. The 2008 season was no exception, and Palin's nomination gave comedians unprecedented fodder for

Tina Fey's (right) resemblance to Sarah Palin (left) made her a natural to spoof the 2008 vice presidential candidate.

Tina Fey and Will Ferrell appear as Sarah Palin and George W. Bush in a Saturday Night Live sketch. Fey's return to SNL to play Sarah Palin made her an even bigger celebrity.

jokes. The combination of her beauty, small-town background, and mangled statements provided comedians with a wealth of material—and no comedian tackled the Sarah Palin issue as well as Tina Fey. In fact, Fey returned to *SNL* to make several appearances as Palin, and these catapulted her career from red-hot to white-hot.

Fey was a natural to play Palin. The actress already resembled the governor—both had dark hair, fair skin, and wore similar glasses. With the right wardrobe, wig, and makeup, *Saturday Night Live* stylists were able to outfit Fey with Palin's trademark upswept hairdo and brightly colored, high-necked skirt suits—and the resemblance was truly remarkable.

By all accounts, Fey's impersonation was dead-on. Fey studied up on imitating Palin's twangy, middle-America accent and hilariously replicated her brand of circuitous logic. In many cases all it took for Fey to deliver a successful parody was to repeat what Palin had said during an interview and change just a few words here and there. For example, a few months before the election, Palin was interviewed several times by *CBS Evening News* anchor Katie Couric. These interviews were a gold mine for Fey's impersonations. For example, when asked about America's financial problems, Palin gave Couric the following incoherent answer:

> That's why I say, I, like every American I'm speaking with, we're ill about this position that we have been put in, where it is the taxpayers looking to bailout. But ultimately, what the bailout does is help those who are concerned about the healthcare reform that is needed to help shore up our economy, helping the—oh, it's got to be all about job creation, too, shoring up our economy and putting it back on the right track. So, healthcare reform and reducing taxes and reining in spending has got to accompany tax reductions and tax relief for Americans. And trade, we have—we've got to see trade as opportunity, not as a competitive, scary thing, but one in five jobs being created in the trade sector today. We've got to look at that as more opportunity. All those things under the umbrella of job creation. This bailout is a part of that.[54]

To impersonate the Alaskan governor, Fey wrote dialogue that closely matched Palin's original words. She played up the governor's stunted sentences and jumps in logic and sprinkled them with comedic elements. She kept many of the same hand and facial gestures the governor had used, lending the performance an additional realistic bent. And above all, she nailed Palin's twangy accent and folksy manner of speaking.

To get in character, Fey worked hard to adopt Palin's distinct accent. "She has a really crazy voice," she told David Letterman when she appeared on his show. "It's a little bit *Fargo*, a little bit Reese Witherspoon in *Election*. I also try and base it on my friend Paula's grandma—a sweet little ol' lady from Joliet, Illinois." To play up Palin's unique manner of speaking, Fey worked with the sketch writers to use words that heavily featured the letter *R*. "She

Sarah Palin

Sarah Palin was born in 1964 in Idaho but her family moved to Wasilla, Alaska, when she was an infant. She spent her early years as a teen beauty queen, placing third in the Miss Alaska competition in 1984. Palin initially worked as a sportscaster for several Anchorage television stations and married her husband, Todd, in 1988.

She became a member of Wasilla's city council from 1992 and 1996, when she was elected the city's mayor. She served as mayor from 1996 to 2002. In 2006 she was elected the governor of Alaska, the youngest person and the first female ever to do so in that state. She did not gain national political prominence, however, until she was tapped in 2008 to be Republican presidential nominee John McCain's running mate. The pair lost the election to President Barack Obama and Vice President Joe Biden.

Palin is known for her folksy style and fiercely Christian values. She has five children, who range in age from 20 years old to 2. In July 2009, Palin resigned as Alaska's governor halfway through her term to pursue other endeavors.

loves those Rs," said Fey. "I think she thinks there's oil in those Rs, she's digging deep."[55] In her rendition of the Couric interview, Fey had the following take on the governor's performance:

> Like every American I'm speaking with, we're ill about this. We're saying, "Hey, why bail out Fanny and Freddie and not me?" But ultimately what the bailout does is, help those that are concerned about the healthcare reform that is needed to help shore up our economy to help . . . uh . . . it's gotta be all about job creation, too. Also, too, shoring up our economy and putting Fannie and Freddy back on the right track and so healthcare reform and reducing taxes and reigning in spending . . . 'cause Barack Obama, y'know . . . has got to accompany tax reductions and tax relief for Americans, also, having a dollar value meal at restaurants. That's gonna help. But one in five jobs being created today under the umbrella of job creation. That, you know. . . . Also. . . .[56]

Americans found the segment funny because Fey used so much of Palin's original dialogue in the parody, and thus cut to the heart of what struck Palin opponents as so ridiculous about her nomination in the first place.

"I Can See Russia from My House!"

Palin gave Fey lots of material over the course of the campaign. For example, when the governor was criticized for having little foreign policy experience, she argued that Alaska's nearness to Russia qualified as such. The claim was silly and exposed as hollow by most observers, including Fey, who made fun of it in a sketch later that week in which she, as Palin, said, "I can see Russia from my house!"[57] In fact, Fey's take on Palin's comment was so popular that for a while, the "I can see Russia from my house!" quote was attributed to Palin on countless blogs and forwarded e-mails.

Fey took another stab at Palin's claims to foreign policy experience by imitating another segment of Palin's interview with Katie Couric. In this section, Couric asked Palin to further explain her foreign policy experience. The conversation went as follows:

Couric: You've cited Alaska's proximity to Russia as part of your foreign policy experience. What did you mean by that?

Palin: That Alaska has a very narrow maritime border between a foreign country, Russia, and on our other side, the land—boundary that we have with—Canada. . . .

Couric: Explain to me why that enhances your foreign policy credentials.

Palin: Well, it certainly does because our—our next door neighbors are foreign countries. They're in the state that I am the executive of. And there in Russia—

Couric: Have you ever been involved with any negotiations, for example, with the Russians?

Palin: We have trade missions back and forth. We—we do—it's very important when you consider even national security issues with Russia . . . where—where do they go? It's Alaska. It's just right over the border. It is—from Alaska that we send those out to make sure that an eye is being kept on this very powerful nation, Russia, because they are right there. They are right next to—to our state.[58]

Again, Fey (with Amy Poehler playing Couric) took a light hand in making fun of the governor's long-winded and somewhat silly answer. In an *SNL* skit that aired a few days after the Couric interview, she kept the message closely linked to the original, adding a few comedic twists:

[Poehler as Couric] On foreign policy, I want to give you one more chance to explain your claim that you have foreign policy experience based on Alaska's proximity to Russia. What did you mean by that?

[Fey as Palin] Well, Alaska and Russia are only separated by a narrow maritime border. You got Alaska here, this right here is water, and this is Russia. So, we keep an eye on them.

[Poehler as Couric] And how do you do that exactly?

[Fey as Palin] Every morning, when Alaskans wake up, one of the first things they do, is look outside to see if there are any Russians hanging around. And if there are, you gotta go up to them and ask, "What are you doing here?" and if they can't give you a good reason, it's our responsibility to say, you know, "Shoo! Get back over there!"[59]

A Household Name

Americans of all political persuasions were electrified by the performances. "Beyond all reasonable doubt, Sarah Fey and Tina Palin are one,"[60] observed one reporter. Said fellow comedian and *SNL* star Darrell Hammond, "I've never seen a better impression. If they put those two on a sonar, they would match up electronically."[61] Indeed, with her performances as Palin, "Tina Fey" became a household name—and at times was even mistaken for the real vice presidential candidate. "It's the most ridiculous, borderline-dangerous thing that the Republican vice-presidential nominee happened to look like the funniest woman working in America,"

A spoof of the vice presidential debate shows Tina Fey as Sarah Palin. People of all political persuasions were dazzled by Fey's performance as Palin.

said *SNL* writer Adam McKay. "What if the next Republican presidential nominee looks exactly like [actor/comedian] Seth Rogen?"[62]

Fey's wildly popular performances led her to be voted one of America's ten most fascinating people by Barbara Walters and also one of the most influential people of the year by *Time* magazine. Fey was catapulted into the national spotlight by her dead-on impression of the Republican vice presidential candidate, and these appearances were credited with shaping the national dialogue about the election and even influencing Americans' votes.

Chapter 4

The Good Girl

In real life, Tina Fey is a lot like many of the characters she writes and plays. She has the moral authority of math teacher Ms. Norbury (her character in *Mean Girls*); the innocence and straitlacedness of fertility-challenged Kate Holbrook (her character in *Baby Mama*); and the professional drive and perseverance of television writer Liz Lemon (her character on *30 Rock*).

A Hard Worker

Whether she is writing or acting, Fey is known as an incredibly hard worker. For example, she took only forty-three days of maternity leave from *Saturday Night Live* when her daughter, Alice, was born in 2005. At the time she said, "I had to get back to work. NBC has me under contract; the baby and I only have a verbal agreement."[63] Although she was joking, clearly something drives Fey to push herself to the extreme edge, taking little time for rest or relaxation.

A typical day in the life of Tina Fey is grueling by anyone's standards. On a normal day of shooting *30 Rock*, for example, Fey only has time to come home, play with her daughter briefly, and put her to bed. Then she starts writing, editing, or looking over other peoples' scripts. When she is not shooting, she might write for ten or twelve hours a day. On other days she might stay up into the wee hours of the night, going over outlines or rewriting her own work. "I don't—and this is not an exaggeration—have

Tina Fey is known for being a hard worker and only took a small amount of time off after having her daughter, Alice.

time to put lotion on," she says of her busy schedule. "If I get enough time in the morning to go to the bathroom and brush my teeth and put on the clothes that I wore the day before, that's it. The idea of putting lotion on my legs, that's not happening."[64]

Fey tends to work on multiple projects simultaneously, which takes a toll on both the writer herself and the people around her. For example, Fey went straight from finishing the first season of *30 Rock* to shooting *Baby Mama*, even though she had to get to work on writing *30 Rock*'s second season of scripts. Some actors bring pets, family members, or stylists to the set of the movie they are filming, but not Fey—while on the set of *Baby Mama*, Fey brought the *30 Rock* writers with her so they could get a jump on writing the show's second season. She took on a similarly hectic schedule when *Mean Girls* was being made—she drove back and forth between Toronto (where *Mean Girls* was shot) and New York, where she was hosting "Weekend Update" on *Saturday Night Live*.

Even when she's working on just one project at a time, Fey demands the most of herself and the people around her. It is common for her to bring writers home with her after a day at the *30 Rock* studio so she can be with her daughter and get work done at the same time. "We continue writing until I can no longer stay awake," she says. "I would be lying if I said there were not tears involved at home occasionally—just occasionally. The life of the working parent is constantly saying, 'This is impossible,' and then you just keep doing it."[65]

Fey expects the people she collaborates with to work as hard as she does. She has a reputation for having very high standards, for both herself and the people around her. "Sometimes people expect that I'm going to be tough," she says. "It's not a bad situation. People treat you better. People are on time."[66] It is well known that Fey is a bit of a perfectionist and likes to monitor the work of the people around her. Says friend and costar Amy Poehler, "Tina likes to be at the top of the mountain, keeping an eye on things."[67] Despite her tough standards and rigid expectations, Fey manages to be well liked by most people with whom she works. One reporter who followed her behind the scenes at *Saturday Night Live* observed the following about her work demeanor: "Fey was considerate and accessible. She solicited a range of opinions, paid earnest compliments. . . . Only every now and then did she turn to a writer and say something like, 'Jesus, how long did it take you to come up with *that*?'"[68]

A Bit of a *Mean Girl*

Since she was a little girl, Fey has exhibited a snarky mean streak. While no one she knows describes her as a mean person, exactly, almost everyone around her recognizes that her humor sometimes has a nasty edge to it. Says one reporter, "Nearly all Fey's colleagues [at *Saturday Night Live*] mentioned her ability to be mean and disarming at the same time. I heard her humor variously described as 'hard-edged,' 'vicious,' and 'cruel.'"[69] Fey does not intend to come off as cruel or unpleasant, though she does admit she possesses an extraordinary gift for coming up with sarcastic comments. "I'm not a mean person, but I have a capacity for it," she admits. "I have the biting comment formed somewhere in the back of my head—like it's in captivity."[70]

Despite her capacity for all things caustic, Fey is actually a very sensitive person and even insecure at times. For example, when it was proposed that she not only write but also star in *30 Rock*, Fey at first hesitated, wondering if she was getting too old for on-camera work or if she were really the person viewers wanted to see for half an hour on their TVs. But then she realized she had to have more confidence in herself and tried to think more like the male comedians she has seen rise to success with their own shows.

"50 Most Beautiful People"

In addition to worrying if she has what it takes to be in front of the camera versus behind the writer's desk, she also remains insecure about her looks. Even though the rest of the world has embraced her as an intelligent sex symbol, Fey herself continues to make self-deprecating jokes and put herself down when complimented by others. For example, when *People* magazine called to tell her they had nominated her as one of the 50 Most Beautiful People of 2003, her first response was to take a shot at herself. She told the person who was calling, "I've been reading the

Jeff Richmond

Tina Fey's husband, Jeff Richmond, is just as talented as his wife. He has acted and produced television but is best known for composing music.

Richmond went to Kent State University, where he worked on the scores of several musicals. He met Fey in Chicago when they worked together in the Second City acting troupe, she as an actor and he as a musician. Shortly after Fey went to work at *Saturday Night Live*, Richmond was hired there as a composer. He left *SNL* in 2006 to compose music for his wife's show, *30 Rock*, where he currently works and has appeared as an extra.

Reporters have often commented on the comfortable relationship enjoyed by Fey and Richmond. Perhaps this is because they dated for seven years before marrying on June 3, 2001. When together, they tend to act and speak with the relaxed intimacy of people who have known each other for a very long time. Even though he is ten years her senior, the two come off as very good friends with a lot in common.

Their favorite pastimes revolve around spending time with their daughter, Alice Zenobia Richmond, who was born September 10, 2005.

Tina Fey and her husband, Jeff Richmond. Richmond is a talented musician.

'50 Most Beautiful People' issue for years, and there's always one person on the list who makes you think, 'Give me a [expletive] break.' This year, I'm proud to be that person."[71]

Likewise, when one interviewer recently asked if she would be happier trading her hectic, work-heavy lifestyle for a day at the beach with a pack of paparazzi photographers snapping illicit shots of her bikini-clad bottom, she sarcastically replied, "Boy, that'd be bad for all parties, because that thing is *gone*."[72] Like many people who have undergone a dramatic physical transformation, Fey has trouble seeing herself as anything other than the awkward nerd she was back in high school. "Tina has remained self-deprecating even as she has glammed up," says friend and *30 Rock* cowriter Kay Cannon. "She'll always see herself as that other, the thing she came from."[73]

Judgmental and Straitlaced

Perhaps in part because of her insecurities, Fey has an overwhelming good-girl morality about her that is evidenced in everything she does. She thinks smoking is disgusting, she rarely drinks, and she has never touched drugs. Her sense of right and wrong was established when she was in high school, when she reserved her meanest jokes and nicknames for the kids who drank, took drugs, cut class, and dressed inappropriately.

As an adult she continues to judge others for what she considers to be inappropriate behavior. She openly disapproves of rude people and will reportedly say something if she sees a person spit on the sidewalk or have too much to drink. She hates people who cut in line or otherwise cheat others to get what they want. "She's pretty monastic at times,"[74] says Poehler, meaning that Fey's behavior can resemble that of a monk or a nun. Fey's husband, Jeff Richmond, agrees. "I don't know if she's judgmental—maybe 'fascinated.' Nah, 'judgmental' is the right word"[75] to describe her.

Fey attributes her reserved character to growing up in the 1980s under the influence of Nancy Reagan's "Just Say No" antidrug campaign. Fey says she took Reagan's instructions literally—and just said no to everything. "I don't enjoy any kind of danger or volatility," she says. "I don't have that kind of 'I love the bad guys'

Despite being nominated by People magazine as one of the 50 Most Beautiful People, Fey still considers herself an awkward nerd.

No Tolerance for Cheating

In addition to looking down upon people who drink and do drugs, Fey also holds a special dislike for people who commit adultery. According to her husband Jeff, Fey regards cheating as one of the worst things a person can do. Fey regards being in a relationship as signing up to agree to certain rules—and has no tolerance for those who break them. If someone is married, she also thinks it is wrong for them to flirt with anyone who is not their spouse. "She has her principles and she sticks to her principles more than anybody I've ever met in my life," says her husband. "She's very black-and-white."

Quoted in Maureen Dowd, "What Tina Wants," *Vanity Fair*, January 2009. www.vanityfair.com/magazine/2009/01/tina_fey200901?currentPage=1.

thing. No, no thank you. I like nice people."[76] Fey exudes this good-girl persona in her home life and hobbies. She is very soft-spoken and likes to sew and bake cookies. A satisfying night for her might include indulging in some cupcakes (her favorite dessert) or maybe a big hunk of cheese. Perhaps as a result of her own personal physical transformation, she loves to watch television shows that deal with renovation, such as cosmetic makeovers and home improvement shows.

When asked by *New York Times* columnist Maureen Dowd what the wildest thing she has ever done is, Fey replied, "Nothing."[77] Fey projects a strict morality onto her projects, too. For example, in *Baby Mama*, when her character, Kate, is persuaded to go out clubbing, she innocently agrees, saying, "[Well,] there is a new ginger body splash I've been dying to try."[78] Likewise, the character she wrote and played in *Mean Girls*, Ms. Norbury, is, as Fey puts it, "the moral compass of the movie."[79] As Fey would like to do in real life, Ms. Norbury helps the movie's mean girls come to terms with their insecurities and encourages them to feel good about themselves, rather than embarrass themselves by wearing inappropriate clothing, too much makeup, or dumbing themselves down to get attention from a guy. In countless other bits and barbs, Fey's devotion to an almost provincial understanding of right and wrong is evident.

Seeking Strong Role Models for Women

It is perhaps a combination of Fey's good-girl mentality, her exceedingly high standards, and her devotion to feminism that causes her to be disappointed with how women are portrayed in society—and with the way many choose to portray themselves. For example, Fey considers plastic surgery a form of mutilation and looks down on women who have it done. She thinks fake tans, face lifts, and enhanced breasts are silly and make women unoriginal and sanitized. Fey feels that celebrities in the sixties and seventies "weren't as homogenized as they are today. But now they're all so fake-looking, and the same kind of fake-looking."[80]

As for the pictures that are taken of her, she will allow some airbrushing and touch-ups to be done. "The most I've changed pictures out of vanity was to edit around any shot where you can see my butt," she says. "I like to look goofy," she explains, "but I also don't want to get canceled because of my big old butt."[81] Since, unlike other actresses, Fey would never consider getting plastic surgery or undergoing Botox, she thinks digitally adjusting certain unflattering pictures is a fair compromise.

Fey reserves an open disregard for young female celebrities who abuse alcohol and drugs and who dress provocatively to get attention. For example, she holds a special hatred for Paris Hilton, considering her to be a bad influence on young girls and women. Fey knows people with teenage daughters who are fascinated by Hilton so she knows firsthand the kind of influence Hilton has on young girls. Fey wishes girls would ignore Hilton altogether. Fey has often made such young female celebrities the target of her cutting, snarky humor. In 2008, in a guest appearance on "Weekend Update," for example, she ragged on

Lindsay Lohan, who has for years captured tabloid headlines with haggard-looking photos and reports about her struggles with eating disorders, drug and alcohol abuse, and promiscuity. Fey reported that Lohan had just re-created an old Marilyn Monroe photo shoot for *New York Magazine* and congratulated the troubled teen star on "continuing to find new and different ways to look old."[82]

Hoping America Will Be "Better than That"

In addition to looking down on the wanton behavior of celebrities, Fey also says she disapproves of the promiscuity and immodesty that has been adopted by many unfamous American girls. She is particularly hostile toward the *Girls Gone Wild* videotapes, which feature college-aged girls flaunting their sexuality for a video camera. "The idea of like, let's get wasted and fake make out with each other to amuse this strange guy" really bothers her, she says. "Ladies, don't show your knockers to [*Girls Gone Wild* creator] Joe Francis. Get your own camera, film your own knockers and get the money."[83] Although Fey is partly joking, she is sincere in her dislike of men whom she says take advantage of women. For this reason, she always advises women to do their own thing with their assets and talents.

Not surprisingly, Fey also hates strip clubs because of the way they objectify women. She considers them to be disrespectful—both to the women on the stage and to the wives and girlfriends of the men who visit them. "I feel like we all need to be better than that," she says. "That industry needs to die, by all of us being a little bit better than that."[84]

Interestingly, however, Fey loves to write parts for stripper characters and to play them in her work. For example, the pilot episode of *30 Rock* shows Fey's character Liz Lemon going to a strip club, getting drunk, and getting onstage to dance with a stripper named Charisma. In another example from a third-season episode of *30 Rock*, Lemon is forced to go to a strip club with her staff. As if to remind both her staff and the audience of what strip clubs are re-

Tina Fey bases many of her acting choices on characters that represent strong role models for women.

ally all about, she says with fake excitement, "Let's go see some naked daughters and moms!"[85] Some speculate that Fey writes such parts as her way of showing how silly and unnecessary the industry really is.

Fey is not only concerned with America's teenagers and young women getting unhealthy messages about sexuality and womanhood —she is also concerned about very young girls, like her daughter,

Alice. As a two-year-old, Alice liked to play with Disney figurines such as princesses. "I think this is ingenious marketing, but that princess thing sets off an alarm bell for me," says Fey. She says she is bothered by the qualities of helplessness or defenselessness such toys impart to kids and is especially upset by the lengths classic female animated characters go to in order to attract men. For example, she is disturbed by the idea "that a girl would really aspire to be the Little Mermaid, a beautiful redhead with no legs who waits for her prince! Who literally gives up her voice! What are we doing? What's going on?"[86]

A Fearful Side

Although she is best known for her boldness, Fey also has a very fearful side to her. In fact, she can at times be an intensely scared person, which probably stems from the slashing attack she suffered as a five-year-old. For example, while all Americans were frightened and haunted by the terrorist attacks of September 11, 2001, Fey was traumatized by them and even considered moving away from New York City as a result.

Fey was also deeply upset later that year when the deadly toxin anthrax was anonymously sent to the *Saturday Night Live* offices. Anthrax is a very serious and potentially deadly disease caused by exposure to a bacterium called *Bacillus anthracis*. She recalls sitting in her dressing room on a Friday, writing copy for that week's "Weekend Update" segment, when she heard on the news that anthrax had been discovered at 30 Rockefeller Plaza, the address of the studios. Without a word to anyone, Fey immediately left the building, hurrying past guest stars, and headed straight for her house, crying the whole way home.

Although all of the people in the building were evacuated, everyone came back—except Fey. She was indescribably struck with fear and was convinced everyone in the building was going to die. She was so shaken up, in fact, that she needed therapy to cope with the event. After talking to a therapist, Fey recognized the connection between her reaction to the anthrax attacks and the attack she suffered as a little girl. "It's the attack out of nowhere," she says. "Something comes out of nowhere, it's horrifying."[87]

Ms. Manners Meets Ms. Palin

Fey's manners were on display even as she took jabs at Republican vice-presidential nominee Sarah Palin. After weeks of enduring Fey's merciless impression of her, Palin finally made arrangements to appear on *Saturday Night Live* in person, and Fey agonized over the meeting. She reportedly told friend Conan O'Brien (host of *The Tonight Show with Conan O'Brien*) that even though she knew it was her job to make fun of Palin, she was nervous about doing it to her face because Palin was first and foremost a human being and a mom.

That is why Fey arranged a skit that minimized the amount of mocking she would have to do of Palin. The sketch featured the real and fake Palins walking silently past each other, looking each other up and down—but that is where the interaction ended. Fey said she wanted to minimize the amount of time they were onscreen together in part because it would highlight the holes in her impression, but also because she was just too uncomfortable to make fun of Palin in person.

Even though much of her career has involved making light of sensational news events, Fey prefers a quieter, calmer world. "I want every day to be the most boring news day ever," she says. "I want every day to be about spelling bee champions and baby basketball. It's better to have no comedy material than a horrific news day."[88] In fact, when she describes her ideal day, it is not very glamorous and bears a resemblance to a typical outing any average American might have: She and her husband would take their daughter to a playground at a nearby park and then go to a restaurant around the corner from their house for burgers, fries, and milkshakes.

Chapter 5

The Future Is Fey's

Fey's already healthy career exploded in 2008 when her wildly popular appearances as Alaska governor Sarah Palin, coupled with the success of her film projects and her television series *30 Rock*, cemented her position as a rare, multifaceted talent in the small world of female comedians.

Truly Political Comedy

It was the Sarah Palin performances that launched Tina Fey to white-hot status in 2008, and to this day people are still discussing what extent her sketches may have influenced the outcome of the presidential election. Indeed, Fey's impersonations of Palin were credited with no less than shaping the national dialogue about the election and even influencing Americans' votes.

Although it cannot be known to what extent the public was affected by the performances or whether they were influenced positively or negatively, surveys show that Americans were in fact impacted. According to one poll conducted by the Pew Research Center in October 2008, the American public was slightly more familiar with Fey's *Saturday Night Live* renditions of Palin than they were with Palin's real media events. For example, 42 percent said they had either seen or heard about Fey's portrayal of Palin on *SNL*, while 41 percent said that they had either seen or heard about Palin's real interview with Katie Couric. Furthermore, after Fey's spoof of Palin's interview with Couric, awareness of and interest in the real

Darrell Hammond, Tina Fey, and Will Ferrell (from left to right) on Saturday Night Live. Fey's impersonations of Sarah Palin are believed to have influenced the national presidential election.

interviews increased. Americans were also much more aware of Fey's sketches than they were of Republican presidential nominee John McCain's campaign appearances made during the same time (only 34 percent said they were aware of these).

Some analysts, such as Lauren Feldman, a communications professor at American University, believe the hype surrounding Fey's performances altered the outcome of the election by cementing negative views about Palin in the public's mind. "The more you see Tina Fey sending up Sarah Palin's style of speech, her folksy mannerisms and her lack of knowledge," said Feldman, "the more those characteristics rise to the top of your mind when you come to listen to the real Sarah Palin, and that influences your assessment of her."[89] Political science professor Jerald Podair agreed. "Presidential impersonators do influence elections," said Podair. "In this one, Tina Fey is well on her way to ruining Sarah Palin's political career."[90] As one reporter writing for the *New York Times* put it, "It could be that the McCain campaign has concluded that what Palin really faces is a Tina Fey problem: Fey's impersonation of Palin has proved so dead-on—and popular—that it has further undermined Palin's plausibility."[91]

Yet others disagreed, taking the "all press is good press" approach to Fey's imitations of Palin. Many thought the sketches actually helped Palin politically by giving her phenomenal exposure. Also, because Palin supporters were so offended by the sketches, they were mobilized to work even harder on her behalf and became even more loyal to her.

Palin and Fey Meet Face-to-Face

Palin's chances in the election were also thought to be helped by her own appearance on *Saturday Night Live* on October 18, 2008. In a much-anticipated broadcast, Palin guest-starred on the show and came face-to-face with Fey-as-Palin. Although it is common for politicians to make appearances on *Saturday Night Live*, most do so to portray a more likeable or casual version of themselves. Palin, however, had already convinced much of America she was both likeable and casual—it was her credentials as a politician she was having trouble with.

But Palin's appearance on *SNL* boosted interest in both the show and the election from people of all political persuasions. Audiences were mesmerized as Palin and her doppelganger walked silently past each other, as identical as mirror images. Palin showed her fantastic sense of humor as she allowed herself to be mocked as "Caribou Barbie" and danced along to a rap about her and her husband that mocked their grizzly Alaskan lifestyle. "Palin on Saturday presented herself as a palate cleanser, or halftime show, for Democrats and Republicans alike," wrote one *New York Times* reporter. "Just two weeks before the election, the Republicans are not pulling out all the stops to frame Palin as a knowledgeable, thoughtful vice president; they are showcasing her as a star."[92]

Not everyone thought that Palin's appearance on the show helped her, though—in fact, the very next day former secretary of state Colin Powell chose to endorse Barack Obama, even though Powell had served in the Republican administration of George W. Bush and was expected by some to endorse the Republican ticket.

"All Those Jokes Were Fair Hits"

Palin herself seemed comfortable with the portrayals of her at the time, saying she thought Tina Fey looked a lot like her and she had been a longtime fan of the actress (in fact, Palin told Fox News that she had once dressed up as Tina Fey for Halloween). She watched the first sketch, which featured Fey as Palin and Poehler as Clinton, from her plane and reportedly laughed out loud.

After she lost the election, however, her opinion about the entertainer's spoofs apparently changed. In a conservative documentary called *How Obama Got Elected*, Palin claimed that Fey spent the election season capitalizing on and even exploiting the public's interest in her. Said Palin, "I did see that Tina Fey was named entertainer of the year . . . that's a little bit perplexing, but it also says a great deal about our society."[93] She also resented the jokes Fey made about her family, saying that she was not aware of them at the time and that they deeply disturbed her. Despite the many deep digs made against Palin, Fey says she has no remorse about the sketches. "I feel clean about it," she says. "All those jokes were fair hits."[94]

Sarah Palin, pictured during an interview, changed her favorable views on Tina Fey's spoofs of her after she lost the election.

Even though the impersonations catapulted her career to heights she had never dreamed, Fey never wanted the sketches to last more than a few weeks. Just before the election, she said: "If she wins, I'm done. I can't do that for four years. And by 'I'm done,' I mean I'm leaving Earth."[95] It was not that Fey did not enjoy playing Palin. But when McCain and Palin lost the election, the demands of Fey's already intense workload and her fear of being typecast into one role led her to feel relieved—at least for professional reasons.

The Awards Come Rolling In

As if 2008 were not already a big year for her, Fey's successful performances as Palin were joined by an astounding number of awards won by *30 Rock*. Although it was slow to gain viewership,

30 Rock swept awards contests in several categories, showing that critics think it is one of the best shows on television today.

Many of its actors have won awards for their performances on the series, and Fey won a 2008 Screen Actors Guild Award for her work. The show also won the Writers Guild of America Award and the award for Best Comedy Series in 2008. That same year the Producers Guild of America awarded the show the Danny Thomas Producer of the Year Award in Episodic Series, and the show also won the Outstanding Achievement in Comedy Award from the Television Critics Association. It also won a Peabody Award in 2008, along with several Golden Globe Awards.

For its second season *30 Rock* broke records when it received seventeen Emmy nominations, making it the most-nominated comedy series for any individual Emmy year. In 2009, *30 Rock* again broke records when its third season was nominated for twenty-two Emmy awards. Fey has won several individual awards for writing specific episodes and for her performance in the series overall.

*Tina Fey accepts an Emmy award for her work as both writer and actress on **30 Rock**.*

Connecting with American Women

The boost from Fey's Palin performances on *SNL*, along with *30 Rock*'s numerous awards, have helped earn the show the popularity and recognition among viewers that critics think it deserves. Fey's character, Liz Lemon, has particularly resonated with female audiences. They connect to her realistic, career-woman lifestyle and the challenges that come along with it. One writer described Lemon as "arguably the most realistic single career woman to appear on TV since Mary Tyler Moore."[96]

Indeed, Lemon's career-driven, chronically single, food-obsessed lifestyle has resonated with many American women in their thirties and forties. Lemon shares all the hallmarks of a woman who has made the tough choices that propel her to success but leave her lonely at the top and at home. For example, the unmarried, childless Lemon prefers a perfect sandwich to a perfect man; her ideal night is to curl up in comfortable clothes after a long day at work with a glass of wine and an enormous plate of cheese. Similar to Kate Holbrook (Fey's character in *Baby Mama*) who throughout her twenties and thirties opted for promotions rather than parenthood, Lemon—like so many of America's career women—has sacrificed her personal life for the success of her professional life. And in doing so she has had to contend with overbearing male colleagues to whom society has been kinder.

It is for all of these reasons that millions of American women now tune in each week to hear observations such as, "No one has it harder in this country today than women," as Lemon says on one episode of *30 Rock*. "It turns out we can't be president. We can't be network news anchors. Madonna's arms look *crazy*."[97] Lemon's sympathy for the physical, professional, and personal stresses put upon America's professional women is at the heart of what makes her relatable and lovable to them.

The Future of Fey

Fey is one of the hardest-working people in show business, and as of 2009 she had no plans to slow down anytime soon. In ad-

Were the Palin Sketches Sexist?

One complaint about Fey's imitations of Palin was that they were sexist. In September 2008 McCain campaign adviser Carly Fiorina came out against the sketch in which Fey imitated Palin while Amy Poehler imitated Hillary Clinton. "The portrait was very dismissive of the substance of Sarah Palin," Fiorina complained. "They were defining Hillary Clinton as very substantive and Sarah Palin as totally superficial. I think that continues the line of argument that is disrespectful in the extreme, and yes, I would say, sexist."[1]

Fey rejected the accusation that her portrayals of Palin were sexist. If anything, she thought the accusations *themselves* were sexist because they painted Palin as a woman who was unable to take a joke in the same way a man would. "The implication was that she's so fragile, which she is not. She's a strong woman," said Fey. "Also, [these accusations are] sexist because, like, who would ever go on the news and say, . . . 'That seemed awful mean to George Bush when [actor] Will Ferrell [played him].'"[2] Fey maintains that all the jokes she wrote about Palin were fair and in the spirit of fun.

1. Quoted in MSNBC, "McCain Camp Calls Fey's Palin Portrayal 'Sexist,'" September 16, 2008. www.msnbc.msn.com/id/26743182.

2. Quoted in Maureen Dowd, "What Tina Wants," *Vanity Fair*, January 2009. www.vanity fair.com/magazine/2009/01/tina_fey200901?currentPage=1.

dition to continuing with *30 Rock*, she had a full plate of projects slated for work and/or release in 2009 and 2010.

One is a Japanese animated film called *Ponyo*, for which she did voice-over work. Ponyo is an adventurous goldfish who wanders away from home. In her travels she meets a five-year-old boy named Sosuke and his mother, Lisa, the character voiced by Fey. In addition to working on *Ponyo*, Fey also worked on the movie *The Invention of Lying*, whose star-studded cast includes Ricky Gervais, Jennifer Garner, Jonah Hill, Jason Bateman, Rob Lowe, and

Tina Fey and Steve Carell hang out backstage after Fey won the Emmy for 30 Rock. In 2009 Fey and Carell began work on the movie Date Night.

Christopher Guest. The movie takes place in an alternate universe in which no one has ever lied, until an enterprising man (Gervais) tells the first lie and changes the world irrevocably. Fey plays the character of Shelley, who is Gervais's disgruntled assistant. *The Invention of Lying* was released in September 2009 to much anticipation.

Also in 2009 Fey began work on a movie called *Date Night*, which was scheduled for release in the spring of 2010. She and comedian Steve Carell (also formerly of the Second City acting troupe) costar as a married couple who try to spice up their relationship by going out on a date, but things end up horribly awry. Said director Shawn Levy, "I wanted to do a relatable, grounded character comedy about marriage and the lengths we go to preserve the spark. Tina and Steve are smart and relatable, and the tone of their comedy perfectly fits this film."[98] Also on Fey's plate was voice-over work for another animated film called *Oobermind* and a series of American Express commercials in which she stars alongside director Martin Scorsese.

Fey also made plans to branch out to a new entertainment medium: books. She had been pursued by several publishing houses for years, but after her Palin appearances so strongly rocked the nation, she was finally contracted by the publishing group Little, Brown Book Group to write a humor book. Details were sparse on the project, but it was reported that the book was neither a memoir nor an autobiography, but a collection of nonfiction humor essays. According to the *New York Observer*, the book deal was worth $6 million, and part of Fey's contract included the stipulation that part of the proceeds would involve a gift to the nonprofit foundation Books for Kids and go toward building six school libraries in underprivileged New York neighborhoods.

Despite her successful forays into movies and books, Fey says she will always be most interested in working on television programs. "My logical brain plan would be to do more writing for movies because it's a friendlier family lifestyle," she says. "But I don't know if I'd be able to stop myself from trying to do TV again."[99] Although she hopes *30 Rock* continues its now-successful run, Fey has already started brainstorming options for what her next series might be about. She thinks it would probably be something concerning parenthood. She does not think she would star in it, but would probably be interested in making cameo appearances every once in a while.

Taking It While She Can Get It

Even though she is currently one of the most sought-after women in show business, fame has not made Fey any less modest or hardworking. Close friends say she is still the type to call before coming over and to pick up coffee for office assistants if she is getting one for herself. When recognized in public she gets shy, embarrassed, and even awkward. "This woman came up to me," she said of a recent encounter with a fan in an electronics store. "She was like, 'You're a great actress.' And I was like, 'Oh, I don't think so, but thank you.' And she said, 'No, I'm asking you, you're an actress, right?' I said, 'Oh, don't worry about it.' All I could think of to say was 'Don't worry about it.'"[100] Perhaps because she spent so many years behind the writer's desk rather than in front of the camera, Fey still has trouble thinking of herself as a famous actress who is likely to be recognized in public.

In addition to being humble, her personal goals for the future are modest. She says she would like to get a slightly bigger apartment in Manhattan so she and her husband can entertain more guests. She might also like to have another child (though given her hectic schedule and the fact that she is approaching forty, she realizes it is probably unlikely).

She would also prefer to keep at bay the kind of white-hot fame she has accrued since the Palin impersonations, because she fears it will interfere with her ability to do the kind of work she really wants to do. She worries that becoming *too* big will cause her to get caught up in worrying about ratings, advertisers, public relations, paparazzi, and other markers of first-class fame that interfere with her true goals: to work hard and make entertaining movies and television shows. "They should draw up an equation: What level of fame do you need to achieve to keep doing what you want? Because you don't want any more than that," she says. Ideally, Fey would like to remain just slightly under Hollywood's radar so she can continue to live her life and do her work. "How do you get to . . . just live your life, make hilarious movies with your friends, and then go home,"[101] she wonders, and she hopes to achieve this kind of balance in her life.

"You Need to Have a Plan"

Yet she also wants to keep working as hard as she can, because she anticipates a day when her brand of humor will be less in demand. She knows that no one stays this busy all of the time and that there is only a window of time in which she will be able to remain this busy. While she is on top of the crowd, she wants to take advantage of the opportunities that her hit television shows, movies, and sketch appearances have afforded her. At the moment studios and production companies cover Fey's expenses, but she anticipates a day when she will have to pay for travel and other expenses herself. But she also hopes that she realizes when her career is over and does not resort to horrible reality shows out of desperation to be on TV.

Fey is also sensitive to the specific challenges that time poses to women in show business. She has commented that very few

Saturday Night Live on Top Again

Fey's appearances as Palin undeniably boosted her career—a New York–based marketing firm estimated that the sketch performances made Fey recognizable by six out of every ten Americans. They also helped *Saturday Night Live* enjoy a surge in its popularity. More than 10 million people tuned in to watch the first Palin sketch in September 2008. *SNL* had not enjoyed an audience of that size since 2001, when people tuned in after the September 11, 2001, attacks to see how the distinctly New York show would handle humor in the aftermath of the crisis.

By Fey's second appearance as Palin, the number of viewers topped 17 million, and even more people tuned in on the Internet. In all, the five sketches of Fey as Palin generated more than 27 million views on NBC.com, and more than 68 million views on video-sharing sites such as YouTube, MySpace, Metacafe, and DailyMotion. During the show on which Palin herself appeared, *SNL* experienced its highest ratings since 1994.

For the second time in her career, it appeared that Fey helped revive *SNL* as a relevant and timely show. Overall, the "Feylin" performances helped boost *SNL*'s ratings by more than 76 percent since the previous year.

Tina Fey appears as a guest on "Late Night with Jimmy Fallon." Fey realizes that her fame may not last forever, but her fans are banking on her being in the spotlight for a long time to come.

actresses are able to have a lifelong career because as they get older, audiences are less interested in seeing them on screen. She has observed there are more roles available for older men than there are for older women and that audiences have a larger tolerance for the older-but-sexy male actor (such as the Harrison Ford, Tommy Lee Jones, or George Clooney types) than for older women. "I think for women especially, you need to have a plan," she says. "I need to have some other ways to generate income, so I don't have to stretch my face or lift the top of my head with surgery or something."[102]

But despite her insecurities and self-deprecating sense of humor, most of Fey's colleagues, friends, and fans think that the beautiful actress has a long time before people tire of her hot teacher glasses and her sexy librarian skirts. And even after Fey reaches the point where she feels too old or unattractive to appear on-screen, it is likely that her many behind-the-scenes talents—including those as a writer, producer, and concept creator—will keep her in demand and in the news for a long time to come.

Notes

Introduction: A Comedian Makes the News

1. Ed Pilkington, "Tina Fey for Vice President!" *Sydney Morning Herald* (Australia), October 23, 2008.

2. Quoted in MSNBC, "Tina Fey 'Leaving Earth' If Palin Wins," October 13, 2008. www.msnbc.msn.com/id/27164 270.

3. Quoted in Kristen Baldwin, "Tina Fey: One Hot 'Mama,'" *Entertainment Weekly*, April 9, 2008. www.ew.com/ew/article/0,,20190281_5,00.html.

Chapter 1: An Improvised Life

4. Quoted in Maureen Dowd, "What Tina Wants," *Vanity Fair*, January 2009. www.vanityfair.com/magazine/2009/01/tina_fey200901?currentPage=1.

5. Quoted in Virginia Heffernan, "Anchor Woman: Tina Fey Rewrites Late-Night Comedy," *New Yorker*, November 3, 2003. www.newyorker.com/archive/2003/11/03/031103 fa_fact.

6. Quoted in David Hiltbrand, "A 'Grounded' Tina Fey Expands Her Territory to Movies," *Philadelphia Inquirer*, April 28, 2004.

7. Quoted in Noel Murray, "Tina Fey," A.V. Club, November 1, 2006. www.avclub.com/articles/tina-fey,14025.

8. Quoted in Dowd, "What Tina Wants," *Vanity Fair*, January 2009.

9. Quoted in Dowd, "What Tina Wants."

10. Quoted in Dowd, "What Tina Wants."

11. Quoted in *30 Rock*, "Fireworks," Season 1, Episode 18, NBC.

12. Quoted in Eric Spitznagel, "Tina Fey," *Believer*, November 2003. www.believermag.com/issues/200311/?read=interview_fey.

13. Quoted in Fox News, "Tina Fey Gets the Last Laugh," April 25, 2004. http://origin.foxnews.com/story/0,2933, 118079,00.html.

14. Quoted in Fox News, "Tina Fey Gets the Last Laugh."

15. Quoted in Spitznagel, "Tina Fey."

16. Quoted in George Everit, "Tina Fey," Suicide Girls.com, May 10, 2004. http://suicidegirls.com/interviews/Tina+Fey.

17. Quoted in Hiltbrand, "A 'Grounded' Tina Fey Expands Her Territory to Movies."

18. Quoted in Heffernan, "Anchor Woman."

19. Quoted in Murray, "Tina Fey."

20. Quoted in Spitznagel, "Tina Fey."

21. Quoted in Heffernan, "Anchor Woman."

22. Quoted in Heffernan, "Anchor Woman."

23. Quoted in Spitznagel, "Tina Fey."

24. Quoted in Spitznagel, "Tina Fey."

Chapter 2: Live from New York, It's Tina Fey

25. Quoted in Heffernan, "Anchor Woman."

26. Quoted in Kelly Tracy, "Funny Girl," *CosmoGirl*, February 2008.

27. Quoted in Heffernan, "Anchor Woman."

28. Quoted in Heffernan, "Anchor Woman."

29. Quoted in Emily Rems, "Mrs. Saturday Night," *Bust*, Spring 2005, p. 42.

30. Quoted in Rems, "Mrs. Saturday Night."

31. Quoted in Rems, "Mrs. Saturday Night."

32. Quoted in Dowd, "What Tina Wants."

33. Quoted in Dowd, "What Tina Wants."

34. Quoted in Dowd, "What Tina Wants."

35. Quoted in Dowd, "What Tina Wants."

36. Quoted in Dowd, "What Tina Wants."

37. Quoted in Dowd, "What Tina Wants."

38. Hiltbrand, "A 'Grounded' Tina Fey Expands Her Territory to Movies."

39. Quoted in Spitznagel, "Tina Fey."

40. Quoted in Dowd, "What Tina Wants."

41. Quoted in Spitznagel, "Tina Fey."

Chapter 3: Writing Her Way to the Top

42. Quoted in Jeff Otto, "IGN Interviews Tina Fey," IGN Movies, April 23, 2004. http://movies.ign.com/articles/508/508797p1.html.

43. *Mean Girls,* Paramount Pictures, 2004.

44. Quoted in Otto, "IGN Interviews Tina Fey."

45. *Mean Girls,* Paramount Pictures, 2004.

46. Robert K. Elder, "Movie Review: 'Mean Girls,'" *Chicago Tribune*, April 28, 2004. www.chicagotribune.com/entertainment/movies/mmx-040430-movies-review-rke-mean girls,0,2750517.story.

47. Roger Ebert, "Mean Girls," *Sun Times* (Chicago), April 30, 2004.

48. Paul Brownfield, "Tina Fey and Amy Poehler Gamble with the Gal-Pal Comedy 'Baby Mama,'" *Los Angeles Times*, April 20, 2008. http://articles.latimes.com/2008/apr/20/entertainment/ca-feypoehler20.

49. Quoted in Baldwin, "Tina Fey."

50. Manohla Dargis, "Learning on the Job About Birthing Babies," *New York Times,* April 25, 2008.

51. Stephanie Zacharek, "Baby Mama," Salon.com, April 23, 2008. www.salon.com/ent/movies/review/2008/04/23/baby_mama.

52. Claudia Puig, "'Baby Mama' Brings Funny to Full Term," *USA Today*, April 25, 2008. www.usatoday.com/life/movies/reviews/2008-04-24-baby-mama_N.htm.

53. Wesley Morris, "A Bundle of Laughs from Two Funny Women," *Boston Globe*, April 25, 2008. www.boston.com/movies/display?display=movie&id=10726.

54. Quoted in Menacham Rosensaft, "We Can't Vote for Sarah Palin If We Can't Understand What She Says," *Huffington Post*, October 1, 2008. www.huffingtonpost.com/menachem-rosensaft/we-cant-vote-for-sarah-pa_b_131015.html.

55. Quoted in Pilkington, "Tina Fey for Vice President!"

56. Quoted in *Saturday Night Live*, "Couric/Palin Open," NBC, September 27, 2008. www.nbc.com/Saturday_Night_Live/video/clips/couric-palin-open/704042.

57. Quoted in *Saturday Night Live*, "Palin/Hillary Open," September 13, 2008. www.nbc.com/Saturday_Night_Live/video/clips/palin-hillary-open/656281.

58. Quoted in CBS News, "Palin on Foreign Policy," September 18, 2008. www.cbsnews.com/stories/2008/09/25/eveningnews/main4479062.shtml?tag=related;wc448138.

59. Quoted in *Saturday Night Live*, "Couric/Palin Open."

60. Pilkington, "Tina Fey for Vice President!"

61. Quoted in Dowd, "What Tina Wants."

62. Quoted in Dowd, "What Tina Wants."

Chapter 4: The Good Girl

63. Quoted in James Kaplan, "Making It All Work," *Parade*, March 9, 2008.

64. Quoted in Karen Heller, "Tina Fey, Star of 'Baby Mama' and the TV Hit '30 Rock,' Says Her Life Is Pretty Good," *Philadelphia Inquirer*, April 21, 2008.

65. Quoted in Kaplan, "Making It All Work."

66. Quoted in Jancee Dunn, "Tina Fey: Funny Girl," *Reader's Digest*, April 2008. www.rd.com/your-america-inspiring-people-and-stories/tina-fey-interview/article54446.html.

67. Quoted in Heffernan, "Anchor Woman."

68. Heffernan, "Anchor Woman."

69. Heffernan, "Anchor Woman."

70. Quoted in Dunn, "Tina Fey."

71. Quoted in Spitznagel, "Tina Fey."

72. Quoted in Baldwin, "Tina Fey."

73. Quoted in Dowd, "What Tina Wants."

74. Quoted in Heffernan, "Anchor Woman."

75. Quoted in Heffernan, "Anchor Woman."

76. Quoted in Dowd, "What Tina Wants."

77. Quoted in Dowd, "What Tina Wants."

78. *Baby Mama*, Universal Pictures, 2008.

79. Quoted in Hiltbrand, "A 'Grounded' Tina Fey Expands Her Territory to Movies."

80. Quoted in Spitznagel, "Tina Fey."

81. Quoted in Dowd, "What Tina Wants."

82. Quoted in *Saturday Night Live*, "Weekend Update," NBC, February 23, 2008.

83. Quoted in Brownfield, "Tina Fey and Amy Poehler Gamble with the Gal-Pal Comedy 'Baby Mama.'"

84. Quoted in Dowd, "What Tina Wants."

85. Quoted in *30 Rock*, "The Natural Order," Season 3, Episode 20, NBC.

86. Quoted in Kaplan, "Making It All Work."

87. Quoted in Dowd, "What Tina Wants."

88. Quoted in Spitznagel, "Tina Fey."

Chapter 5: The Future Is Fey's

89. Quoted in Pilkington, "Tina Fey for Vice President!"

90. Quoted in Jeremy Olshan, "Palin Falls Prey to Fey," *New York Post*, October 13, 2008. www.nypost.com/seven/10132 008/news/politics/palin_falls_prey_to_fey_133371.htm.

91. Alessandra Stanley, "On 'SNL' It's the Real Sarah Palin, Looking Like a Real Entertainer," *New York Times*, October 20, 2008. www.nytimes.com/2008/10/20/arts/20iht-20watch.17101587.html.

92. Stanley, "On 'SNL' It's the Real Sarah Palin, Looking Like a Real Entertainer."

93. Quoted in John Zeigler, director, *Media Malpractice: How Obama Got Elected and Palin Was Targeted*, How Obama Got Elected.com. http://howobamagotelected.com.

94. Quoted in Dowd, "What Tina Wants."

95. Quoted in MSNBC, "Tina Fey 'Leaving Earth' If Palin Wins."

96. Baldwin, "Tina Fey."

97. Quoted in *30 Rock*, "Believe in the Stars," Season 3, Episode 2. NBC.

98. Quoted in Michael Fleming, "Carell, Fey Ready for 'Date Night,'" *Variety*, August 14, 2008. www.variety.com/article/VR1117990581.html?categoryid=13&cs=1.

99. Quoted in Baldwin, "Tina Fey."

100. Quoted in Baldwin, "Tina Fey."

101. Quoted in Baldwin, "Tina Fey."

102. Quoted in Kaplan, "Making It All Work."

1970
Tina Fey is born on May 18 to Donald and Jeanne Fey.

1975
Fey suffers an anonymous slashing incident that scars her from the corner of her mouth to her cheek on the left side of her face.

1988
Fey graduates from Upper Darby High School.

1992
Fey graduates from the University of Virginia.

1994
Fey joins Second City's touring ensemble.

1997
Fey joins *Saturday Night Live* as a writer.

1999
Fey becomes head writer on *Saturday Night Live*, the first female to do so in the show's history.

2000
Fey is put on camera as a host for "Weekend Update," reviving the segment.

2000–2004
Fey hosts "Weekend Update" with coanchor Jimmy Fallon.

2001
Fey is named one of *Entertainment Weekly's* Entertainers of the Year.

2001
Fey shares a Writers Guild Award for her work on *Saturday Night Live's* twenty-fifth anniversary special.

2001

On June 3 Fey marries Jeff Richmond, the musical composer on *Saturday Night Live*.

2002

Fey helps *Saturday Night Live* win an Emmy for outstanding writing—an award it had not received since 1989.

2002

Fey lands at number 80 on *Maxim* magazine's list of 100 Sexiest Women.

2003

Fey is listed among *People* magazine's 50 Most Beautiful People of the Year, a feat she will repeat in 2006, 2008, and 2009.

2003

Fey is credited with helping *Saturday Night Live* attract more viewers than any other late-night show on the air at the time.

2004

Fey hosts "Weekend Update" with coanchor Amy Poehler, making it the first time in the show's history that two women have anchored the segment; releases *Mean Girls*.

2005

Fey gives birth to her daughter, Alice, on September 10.

2006

Fey leaves *Saturday Night Live* to produce, write, and star in a new comedy series, *30 Rock*; the first episode airs on October 11.

2007

Fey is once again named one of *Entertainment Weekly's* Entertainers of the Year; wins a Writers Guild of America Award for her writing on *Saturday Night Live*; *30 Rock* wins an Emmy for Outstanding Comedy Series.

2008

Fey is named Entertainer of the Year by the Associated Press; comes in as *Entertainment Weekly's* first-place Entertainer of the Year; is selected by Barbara Walters as one of America's 10 Most

Fascinating People of the year; Fey's Sarah Palin sketches help boost *Saturday Night Live's* ratings to heights it had not enjoyed since 2001 and 1994; *30 Rock* and Fey win three Emmys: one for Outstanding Comedy Series, one for Outstanding Actress in a Comedy Series, and one for Outstanding Writing for a Comedy Series; Fey wins a Golden Globe Award for Best Actress in a Television Comedy; wins a Screen Actors Guild Award for Outstanding Performance by a Female Actor in a Comedy Series for her work on *30 Rock*; *30 Rock* wins a Writers Guild of America Award for Outstanding Comedy Series; Fey releases *Baby Mama*.

2009

Fey is listed in *Rolling Stone* magazine's annual list of 100 People Who Are Changing America; signs a $6 million book contract with Little, Brown Book Group to publish a book of humor essays; wins two Golden Globe Awards for *30 Rock*—one for Best Performance by an Actress in a Television Series and one for Best Television Series; wins a Producers Guild of America Award for Producer of the Year Award in Episodic Comedy; wins two Screen Actors Guild awards for her work on *30 Rock*; wins another Writers Guild of America Award for her writing on *30 Rock*.

For More Information

Books

Lorenzo Benet, *Trailblazer: An Intimate Biography of Sarah Palin.* New York: Threshold Editions, 2009.

Tom Davis, *39 Years of Short-Term Memory Loss: The Early Days of SNL from Someone Who Was There.* New York: Grove, 2009.

Kaylene Johnson, *Sarah: How a Hockey Mom Turned the Political Establishment Upside Down.* Carol Stream, IL: Tyndale House, 2008.

James A. Miller and Tom Shales, *Live from New York: An Uncensored History of Saturday Night Live, as Told by Its Stars, Writers and Guests.* Newport Beach, CA: Back Bay, 2003.

Jay Mohr, *Gasping for Airtime: Two Years in the Trenches of Saturday Night Live.* New York: Hyperion, 2005.

Periodicals

Howard Gensler, "The Mover & Shaker in This Election? Tina Fey!" *Philadelphia Daily News*, October 14, 2008.

Karen Heller, "Tina Fey, Star of 'Baby Mama' and the TV Hit '30 Rock,' Says Her Life Is Pretty Good," *Philadelphia Inquirer*, April 21, 2008.

James Kaplan, "Making It All Work," *Parade*, March 9, 2008.

Rick Kissell, "Peacock's 'Rock' Solid," *Variety*, April 6, 2009.

Yael Kohen, "We'll Show You Who's Funny," *Marie Claire*, April 2009.

Ed Pilkington, "Tina Fey for Vice President!" *Sydney Morning Herald* (Australia), October 23, 2008.

Emily Rems, "Mrs. Saturday Night," *Bust,* Spring 2004.

Brian Steinberg, "Can Brand Fey Get Any Bigger? You Betcha," *Advertising Age*, May 18, 2009.

Kelly Tracy, "Funny Girl," *CosmoGirl*, February 2008.

Internet Sources

Alec Baldwin, "The 2009 100: Tina Fey," *Time*, 2009. www.time.com/time/specials/packages/article/0,28804,1894410_1893836_1893831,00.html.

Kristen Baldwin, "Tina Fey: One Hot 'Mama,'" *Entertainment Weekly*, April 9, 2008. www.ew.com/ew/article/0,,20190 281_5,00.html.

Paul Brownfield, "Tina Fey and Amy Poehler Gamble with the Gal-Pal Comedy 'Baby Mama,'" *Los Angeles Times*, April 20, 2008. http://articles.latimes.com/2008/apr/20/entertainment/ca-feypoehler 20.

Maureen Dowd, "What Tina Wants," *Vanity Fair*, January 2009. www.vanityfair.com/magazine/2009/01/tina_fey200901?curr entPage=1.

Jancee Dunn, "Tina Fey: Funny Girl," *Reader's Digest*, April 2008. www.rd.com/your-america-inspiring-people-and-stories/tina-fey-interview/article54446.html.

George Everit, "Tina Fey," Suicide Girls, May 10, 2004. http://suicidegirls.com/interviews/Tina+Fey.

Fox News, "Tina Fey Gets the Last Laugh," April 25, 2004. http://origin.foxnews.com/story/0,2933,118079,00.html.

A.J. Jacobs, "Tina Fey, Make Us Laugh," *Esquire*, May 2008. www.esquire.com/print-this/tina-fey-0508.

Wesley Morris, "A Bundle of Laughs from Two Funny Women," *Boston Globe*, April 25, 2008. www.boston.com/movies/display ?display=movie&id=10726.

Noel Murray, "Tina Fey," A.V. Club, November 1, 2006. www.avclub.com/articles/tina-fey,14025.

National Public Radio, "Tina Fey: Sarah Palin and 'Saturday Night' Satire," November 3, 2008. www.npr.org/templates/story/ story.php?storyId=96494481.

Jeff Otto, "IGN Interviews Tina Fey," IGN Movies, April 23, 2004. http://movies.ign.com/articles/508/508797p1.html.

Amy Poehler, "Tina Fey on Top," *Marie Claire*, 2008. www.marieclaire.com/celebrity-lifestyle/celebrities/interviews/ tina-fey-amy-poehler-interview.

Eric Spitznagel, "Tina Fey," *Believer*, November 2003. www.believer mag.com/issues/200311/?read=interview_fey.

Jacques Steinberg, "Tina Fey's Brash Bid for Prime Time," *New York Times*, April 6, 2006. www.nytimes.com/2006/04/06/arts/ television/06fey.html?_r=1.

Web Sites

Baby Mama (www.babymamamovie.net). The official site for *Baby Mama* includes behind-the-scenes video of the making of the movie, excerpts of interviews with Tina Fey and Amy Poehler, and special facts about the other cast members.

Mean Girls (www.meangirls.com/indexflash.html). The official site for *Mean Girls* features articles, games, and downloads related to the movie.

Saturday Night Live, NBC (www.nbc.com/Saturday_Night_Live). Videos of Tina Fey can be downloaded from the *Saturday Night Live* Web site. Videos available for download include Fey playing Sarah Palin and appearing on the "Weekend Update" segment.

30 Rock (www.nbc.com/30_Rock). News, merchandise, and downloadable videos from Tina Fey's hit show, *30 Rock*.

Tina-Fey.org (www.tina-fey.org). A comprehensive Tina Fey information source, with lots of breaking news reports and more than eight thousand images of the actress/writer.

Picture Credits

Cover image: © Lucas Jackson/Corbis
AP Images, 14, 18, 74
Broadway Video/The Kobal Collection/Bailey, K.C., 43
Business Wire/Getty Images, 21
CBS Photo Archive/Getty Images, 13
Djamilla Rosa Cochran/WireImage/Getty Images, 54
Columbia Pictures/Gemma La Mana/AP Images, 25
Dana Edelson/NBCU Photo Bank via AP Images, 10, 32, 34, 46, 67, 78
Dana Edelson/NBC via AP Images, 51
Michael Germana/UPI/Landov, 37
Eric Liebowitz/NBCU Photo Bank via AP Images, 41
Mathew Imaging/WireImage/Getty Images, 57
Mary Ellen Matthews/NBCU Photo Bank via AP Images, 29
NBCU Photo Bank via AP Images, 31
Paramount/The Kobal Collection/Gibson, Michael, 39
Robert Pitts/Landov, 26
Reuters/Landov, 45
Nicole Revilli/NBCU Photo Bank via AP Images, 59
Bill Roth/MCT/Landov, 70
Jim Ruymen/UPI/Landov, 71
Virginia Sherwood/NBC NewsWire via AP Images, 63

Lauri S. Friedman earned her bachelor's degree in religion and political science from Vassar College in 1999. She is the founder of LSF Editorial, a writing and editing business in San Diego. Friedman lives in Ocean Beach, California, with her husband, Randy, and their yellow lab, Trucker. In her spare time she enjoys cooking, traveling, playing games and music, and watching Tina Fey movies.